AS/A-LEVEL YEAR 1

STUDENT GUIDE

Edexcel

Economics A

Theme 1

Introduction to markets and market failure

Mark Gavin

PHILIP ALLAN FOR
HODDER
EDUCATION
AN HACHETTE UK COMPANY

Philip Allan, an imprint of Hodder Education, an Hachette UK company, Blenheim Court, George Street, Banbury, Oxfordshire OX16 5BH

Orders

Bookpoint Ltd, 130 Milton Park, Abingdon, Oxfordshire OX14 4SB

tel: 01235 827827

fax: 01235 400401

e-mail: education@bookpoint.co.uk

Lines are open 9.00 a.m.–5.00 p.m., Monday to Saturday, with a 24-hour message answering service. You can also order through the Hodder Education website: www.hoddereducation. co.uk

© Mark Gavin 2015

ISBN 978-1-4718-4336-5

First printed 2015

Impression number 5

Year 2018 2017

This Guide has been written specifically to support students preparing for the Edexcel AS and A Level Economics A (Theme 1) examinations. The content has been neither approved nor endorsed by Edexcel and remains the sole responsibility of the author.

Typeset by Integra Software Services Pvt. Ltd., Pondicherry, India

Printed in Dubai

Hachette UK's policy is to use papers that are natural, renewable and recyclable products and made from wood grown in sustainable forests. The logging and manufacturing processes are expected to conform to the environmental regulations of the country of origin.

Contents

■ Getting the most from this book

Exam tips

Advice on key points in the text to help you learn and recall content, avoid pitfalls, and polish your exam technique in order to boost your grade.

Knowledge check

Rapid-fire questions throughout the Content Guidance section to check your understanding.

Knowledge check answers

1 Turn to the back of the book for the Knowledge check answers.

Summaries

■ Each core topic is rounded off by a bullet-list summary for quick-check reference of what you need to know.

Exam-style questions

Commentary on the questions

Tips on what you need to do to gain full marks, indicated by the icon (e)

Sample student answers

Practise the questions, then look at the student answers that follow.

Commentary on sample student answers

Find out how many marks each answer would be awarded in the exam and then read the comments (preceded by the icon (e)) following each student answer. Annotations that link back to points made in the student answers show exactly how and where marks are gained or lost.

Questions & Answers

(g) Discuss measures the government and monetary authorities could take to limit the growth in house prices. [20 marks]

(e) The command phrase 'discuss' invites you to consider the effectiveness of various measures to limit house price growth. It mentions 'monetary authorities' so that it is possible to refer to the role of the bank of England in raising interest rates. Government measures could include abolishing the 'hep to buy scheme', higher Stamp duties on buying property and subsidies to build more social housing. There are 14 knowledge, application and analysis marks available and, 6 evaluation marks to gain.

Student answer

(a) UK average house prices have increased by £150,000 between 2000 and 2013, a huge 150% increase (a) On the demand side, rising incomes, immigration from Eastern Europe and record low interest rates are the causes. Rising real incomes and record low interest rates mean the monthly repayments on house loans are more affordable and so this encourages home ownership. The rise in immigration has put added pressure on a limited housing stock and so driven up its price (b) The diagram shows the demand for housing increasing from D1 to D2 and price increasing from P1 to P2 (c)

(e) 5/5 marks awarded. (a) The student explicitly refers to the data concerning the rise in house prices (1 mark). (b) Three demand side reasons are given for the rise in house prices with some development (1+1 marks). (c) A relevant diagram is shown depicting an increase in demand and higher equilibrium price (1+1 marks).

(b) (a) Price elasticity of supply refers to the responsiveness of supply to the change in the price of a good. Information in the extract indicates that supply of new housing is likely to be price inelastic (where the proportional rise in supply is less than the proportional rise in price.

(b) There appear to be three constraints on supply; first the tight planning regulations on building new housing, especially in urban areas. It takes a long time for developers to gain approval for building new homes and often there are objections by local residents who want to maintain access to open spaces; second, the extract refers to a shortage of skilled building workers such as bricklayers and plumbers – it means developers have to offer high wages and wait for more people to be trained before responding to increased house prices; third, there is a shortage of building materials which further delays the ability of developers to respond to rising house prices. It increases the average time taken to build housing.

(e) 5/5 marks awarded. (a) The student defines price elasticity of supply and explains the meaning of price inelastic supply. It is useful to make it clear to the examiner the meaning of both terms as marks are available. Quite often the latter is missed out in student answers (1+1 marks). (b) Three reasons are offered to

■ About this book

The aim of this guide is to help you prepare for the Edexcel AS and A Level Economics Paper 1 examinations. It includes all of the topics required for the AS exam Paper 1 'Introduction to markets and market failure' (code 8EC0/01) and some of the topics for the A Level exam Paper 1 'Markets and business behaviour' (code 9EC0/01). The concepts and models covered in this guide also directly feed into the synoptic A Level exam Paper 3 'Microeconomics and macroeconomics' (code 9EC0/03).

This guide should be used as a supplement for a taught course along with textbooks and other materials recommended by your teacher. There are two sections:

- The **Content Guidance** section summarises the specification content of Theme 1 required for both the AS and A Level economics syllabus. Theme 1, 'Introduction to markets and market failure', is based on the price mechanism model which underpins the whole syllabus. Theme 1's content comprises four main topics and a summary of key points is provided during and at the end of each one in this guide.
- The **Questions & Answers** section provides guidance on how to answer both the AS exam Paper 1 and the A Level exam Paper 1. It includes multiple-choice and short-answer questions, data response questions and extended open-ended questions. It also includes student answers and comments on how to improve performance.

Specification

The AS Economics specification is structured into two themes and consists of two exam papers, one on each theme. The first theme is 'Introduction to markets and market failure', which corresponds with exam Paper 1 of the same name. The second theme is 'The UK economy: performance and policies', which corresponds with exam Paper 2 of the same name. Note this guide prepares students for exam Paper 1.

The A Level Economics specification is structured into four themes and consists of three exam papers. In addition to the two AS themes, there is Theme 3 'Business behaviour and the labour market' and theme 4 'A global perspective'.

The A Level exam Paper 1, 'Markets and business behaviour' tests models and concepts from Themes 1 and 3. Consequently, it is important to study both themes ('Introduction to markets and market failure' and 'Business behaviour and the labour market') in preparation for taking exam Paper 1.

Exam format

The AS exam Paper 1 'Introduction to markets and market failure' has two sections. Section A comprises five compulsory multiple-choice and short-answer questions; section B comprises one data response question broken down into a number of parts, the last being an open-response question which offers students a choice from two. The time allowed for the examination is 1 hour and 30 minutes.

The A Level exam Paper 1 'Markets and business behaviour' has three sections. Section A comprises five compulsory multiple-choice and short-answer questions; section B comprises one compulsory data response question broken down into a number of parts; section C comprises one extended open-response question which offers students a choice from two. The time allowed for the examination is 2 hours.

Note that the A Level exam Paper 1 requires students to answer questions from Theme 1 'Introduction to markets and market failure' and Theme 3 'Business behaviour and the labour market'. Students are required to learn the models and concepts from both themes in preparation for the exam. You are therefore advised to obtain the accompanying student guide in this series, 'Business behaviour and the labour market', which provides further guidance on the content and exam questions for Theme 3.

Content Guidance

■ The nature of economics

Economics as a social science

Economics is a social science, which means it is concerned with the study of human behaviour. It investigates how scarce resources are allocated to provide for unlimited human wants. Economists develop models which attempt to simplify and improve our understanding of how consumers and producers behave. These models include assumptions — for example, consumers aim to maximise satisfaction or utility when spending their income. Similarly, producers aim to maximise profits from the goods and services they make and sell. Economic models are judged upon their ability to explain and predict consumer and producer behaviour, even when the assumptions of such models are unrealistic.

Thinking like an economist requires use of the *ceteris paribus* assumption. It means 'all other things being equal' or 'all other things remaining the same'. This assumption is needed since economists cannot test models in scientifically controlled laboratory conditions. For example, a sweet shop may cut the price of Mars bars and find that more are demanded or purchased. This leads the construction of a demand curve depicting an inverse relationship between the price and quantity purchased of a good. However, we have to assume that other things remain the same — for example, the level of consumer income, advertising and the price of other types of sweets. Otherwise, a change in any one of these factors could be the cause of more Mars bars being demanded.

> **Economics** The allocation of scarce resources to provide for unlimited human wants.

> **Ceteris paribus** 'All other things being equal'.

Positive and normative economic statements

Positive economics

Positive economics is concerned with facts and is value-free. It is a scientific approach to the discipline, where economists explain the outcome of a particular policy, but are not expected to take sides. Positive statements can be tested as true or false by referring to the facts.

An example of a **positive statement** is: 'The increase in the national minimum wage from £6.31 to £6.50 per hour in October 2014 will cause unemployment.' It is possible to check the facts and see whether this increase does cause unemployment or not. The statement can be accepted as true or rejected as false.

Normative economics

Normative economics is concerned with value judgements and is a non-scientific approach to the discipline. A normative statement is an expression that something is right or wrong, so it often includes the words *ought*, *should*, *fair*, *unfair*, *better* or *worse*.

> **Positive economics statement** Based on facts which can be tested as true or false and are value-free.

> **Exam tip**
>
> Use the term 'value judgement' rather than 'opinion' when explaining a normative economic statement.

An example of a **normative statement** is: 'The reduction in the UK top rate of income tax from 50% to 45% is unfair.' The term 'unfair' is a value judgement which one can agree or disagree with. It is not possible to prove or disprove it, but rather, it depends upon the values held by individuals.

Role of value judgements in economic decision making and policy

Value judgements have a major influence on economic decision making for consumers and producers. Personal preferences, beliefs and subjective assessment underpin normative economics. For example, a highly cautious individual may prefer to save more of his or her income in a pension fund rather than increase current spending on consumer goods; similarly, a producer prone to taking high risks may prefer to spend cash reserves on developing new goods rather than have a safety net for unanticipated future events.

Value judgements also have a major role in government policy making. For example, a government may prefer to cut income tax rather than increase expenditure on healthcare provision. This could be due to an underlying preference for the operation of free market forces rather than more government intervention in an economy.

The economic problem

The economic problem is based on **scarcity**. Scarcity arises because there are insufficient resources to provide for everyone's wants. It occurs in all economies, since resources are finite compared to human material wants. Scarcity is obvious in countries that face famine or drought, where insufficient food or water is available to meet everyone's needs. However, scarcity also exists in wealthy countries, since not all human material wants can be satisfied.

Scarcity means we have to make choices over the use of our limited resources to provide for our material wants. Some crucial decisions have to be made over what, how and for whom to produce. These decisions are faced by consumers, producers and the government. Once a decision has been made about what to use a resource for, opportunity cost arises.

Opportunity costs to economic agents

Opportunity cost refers to the value of the next best alternative forgone. Consumers, producers and government all face opportunity cost.

A consumer may have £25 available to spend on a meal at a restaurant or on the next best thing, which is a new T-shirt. The individual cannot buy both at the same time. If the consumer chooses to buy a meal then the opportunity cost is forgoing the new t-shirt.

A firm may have £50,000 available to invest in a new machine or to invest in a training programme for employees. The managers have to make a choice over the best use of the funds.

A government may have an extra £100 million of tax revenue. It might use this to build a new hospital but, in doing so, forgoes the building of a large school, considered to be the next best alternative.

Normative economics statement Based on value judgements which cannot be tested as true or false.

Exam tip

Always use the information provided to explain why a statement is normative: for example, normative statements are often characterised by value-laden words such as *fair, unfair, better, worse, should* and *ought*.

Scarcity There are finite resources compared to infinite human wants, so choices have to be made about how to use those resources.

Opportunity cost The value of the next best alternative forgone.

Knowledge check 1

What is the opportunity cost of you staying on at school or college to study A Levels?

Renewable and non-renewable resources

Resources, or factors of production, are inputs used in the production of goods and services. They are finite and can be classified into four types: land, labour, capital and enterprise.

A **renewable resource** is one whose stock level can be replenished naturally over a period of time. Such resources include solar energy, wind power, tidal power, fish, timber and soil. However, renewable resources may decline over time if they are consumed at a faster rate than the environment can replenish them. They require careful management, to avoid such things as deforestation and soil erosion.

A **non-renewable resource** is one whose stock level decreases over time as it is consumed. These resources include fossil fuels such as coal, oil and gas. They also include commodities such as steel, copper and aluminium. It is possible to reduce the rate of decline of non-renewable resources through recycling and the development of substitutes. The price mechanism also has a role to play in reducing the rate of consumption via higher prices.

Production possibility frontiers

A production possibility frontier shows the maximum potential level of output for two goods or services that an economy can achieve when all its resources are fully and efficiently employed, given the level of technology available. It can be used to illustrate scarcity and opportunity cost.

Movement along a production possibility frontier

Figure 1 shows the production possibility frontier of an economy with capital and consumer goods. **Consumer goods** directly provide satisfaction or utility to consumers. They are wanted for their own sake rather than for what they produce. Examples include clothing, food, drink, a holiday and iPhones. **Capital goods** are used to produce more consumer goods and services. Generally, they provide satisfaction to consumers indirectly. Examples include machinery, office blocks, training of workers and factories.

Initially, the economy is at point Z. To increase the production of capital goods by 20 units and move to point W, there is an opportunity cost of 30 units of consumer goods.

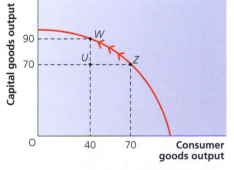

Figure 1 Production possibility frontier

Renewable resource
A resource whose stock level can be replenished naturally over a period of time.

Non-renewable resource A resource whose stock level decreases over time as it is consumed.

Consumer good A good, such as a chocolate bar, that directly provides utility to consumers. It is wanted for the satisfaction it gives.

Capital good A good that is used to produce consumer goods or services, such as a machine that helps make chocolate bars. It is wanted not for its own sake, but rather for the consumer goods and services it can produce.

The movement from *Z* to *W* increases the rate of economic growth, since capital goods are crucial for increasing production. Economic growth can be shown by an outward shift of the production possibility frontier. However, the loss of 30 units of consumer goods means that current living standards will fall in order to enable future living standards to rise at a faster rate.

If the economy is located at any point on its **production possibility frontier**, there is an efficient allocation of resources, since none are being wasted. However, if the economy is located within its production possibility frontier, there is an inefficient allocation of resources as not all are being used. At position *U* it is possible to increase production of both consumer and capital goods, by utilising unemployed resources. Since nothing is given up in return, there is no opportunity cost.

The shape of production possibility frontiers — curves and straight lines

A typical production possibility frontier is bowed to the origin and shows that, as more of one good is produced, an increasing amount of the other good is forgone. The opportunity cost rises. This is because not all resources are as efficient as other resources in the production of both goods. Diminishing returns set in.

A good example is the use of agricultural land in East Anglia and southwest England. We can assume that farmland can be used either for growing wheat or for livestock production. East Anglia has highly fertile and light soils with suitable rainfall for growing wheat. Output per acre is very high. However, as we move towards the southwest, the soil becomes too heavy and rainfall too high for growing wheat. Instead, livestock farming is far more productive per acre. If farmland in the southwest were converted to wheat production, yields would be very low and would be achieved only at a cost of forgoing considerable livestock output.

Shifts in the production possibility frontier

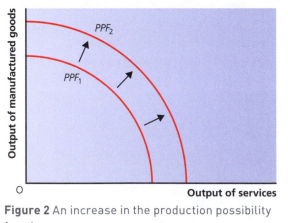

Figure 2 An increase in the production possibility frontier

A country's production potential may increase over time, which is shown in Figure 2 by an outward shift in its production possibility frontier. This represents economic growth and there are a number of possible causes: for example, an increase in the

Production possibility frontier The maximum potential output of a combination of goods an economy can achieve when all its resources are fully and efficiently employed, given the current level of technology.

Knowledge check 2

How might opportunity cost be shown on a production possibility frontier?

Exam tip

Always define key economic concepts in short-answer and data-response questions. Marks are always awarded for this.

Exam tip

Be prepared to annotate or draw a diagram of a production possibility frontier when answering short-answer and data-response questions on this concept. Marks are usually available for this.

quantity or quality of resources; the expansion of further and higher education and government training schemes; or an increase in investment and the development of new technology.

Occasionally the production possibility frontier may shift inwards towards the origin, indicating a decrease in the potential output of an economy. This may be caused by war or a natural disaster where many resources are destroyed. In 2011 an earthquake and the tsunami it caused devastated coastal areas of Japan, reducing its productive capacity.

Specialisation and the division of labour

Specialisation occurs when an individual, a firm, a region or a country concentrates on the production of a limited range of goods and services. The advantages of specialisation are that it increases productivity and living standards across the world. The UK specialises in the production of medicinal drugs, aircraft manufacture, tourism, and financial and business services. These goods and services can then be traded for other goods and services produced by other countries. It leads to a higher level of global output and higher living standards.

Specialisation can have disadvantages, notably when demand for a good or service falls, leading to a significant increase in structural unemployment. Also, a country specialising in the production and export of minerals may face problems of resource depletion. Another problem relates to the price at which goods are sold: for example, many developing countries face an unfavourable rate of exchange, selling their commodities at a low price compared to the goods they purchase from overseas.

The **division of labour** is one form of specialisation, where individuals concentrate on the production of a particular good or service. Production is broken down into a series of tasks, conducted by different workers. For example, house construction involves a range of specialist labour, including architects, surveyors, bricklayers, carpenters and electricians. Adam Smith, the first ever professor of economics, writing in the eighteenth century, explained division of labour by referring to production in a pin factory. He explained that if pin production were broken down into 18 different specialist tasks, each carried out by a different worker, output of pins would increase by 2,000% compared to a situation where each worker had to carry out all the tasks involved.

Advantages of the division of labour

The major advantage is increased productivity (higher output per worker per hour), which leads to higher living standards. Increased productivity helps to reduce the cost per unit of output and so increases the efficiency of resources. The reasons for increased productivity include:

- A worker becoming highly skilled in a task due to repetition (e.g. a tyre fitter in a garage).
- No time is wasted in moving from one job to another (e.g. a packer on a sandwich production line).
- Capital equipment can be used continuously in production (e.g. the machinery on a motor vehicle production line).

Knowledge check 3

What is the state of the economy if it is operating at a point within its production possibility frontier?

Knowledge check 4

Outline the factors which might lead to an outward shift of the production possibility frontier for a country.

Specialisation When an individual, firm, region or country concentrates on the production of a limited range of goods and services.

Division of labour The specialisation of workers on specific tasks in the production process.

- Less time is required to train workers for specific tasks.
- There is more choice of jobs for workers and they can specialise in the tasks they are most suited to (e.g. a person who likes rock climbing might specialise in work as an outdoor pursuits leader).

Exam tip

Be careful not to confuse an increase in total production costs with a decrease in cost per unit of output. Specialisation will typically increase total production costs for a firm, since it is likely to increase total output, requiring more raw materials and machinery. However, it also leads to a reduction in the cost per unit of output, since workers become more productive.

Disadvantages of the division of labour

- Repetition creates monotony and boredom. There could be a high turnover of staff, leading to increased recruitment and selection costs.
- Breaking down production into different tasks makes it easier to replace skilled workers with machines, leading to structural unemployment, such as motor vehicle welders being replaced by robots, or supermarket cashiers being replaced with self-service scanning machines.
- Specialisation creates interdependence in production. If one group of workers goes on strike, it could halt production across the whole industry. For example, when train drivers call a one-day stoppage, they disrupt the work of guards and ticket inspectors, as well as that of many commuters.

Knowledge check 5

Why does the division of labour increase productivity or output per head?

The functions of money

Money is anything that is generally acceptable in the payment of a good or service, or of a debt. Money comes in various forms, largely in cash and bank deposits. Advances in technology mean we are moving towards a cashless society where most payments occur through debiting and crediting bank accounts. The development of money enabled specialisation and trade to grow, leading to the sophisticated economies of today. It is crucial that people have confidence in the money used; otherwise it will lose its general acceptability for making transactions. Once this happens, it ceases to be money. A recent example of this problem arose in Zimbabwe where the government printed off too many Zim dollars, leading to hyperinflation and the currency becoming worthless.

Money Anything that is generally acceptable in the payment of a good or service, or of a debt.

There are four functions of money:

- *Medium of exchange*. It enables the buying and selling of products, making exchange easier. Money eliminates the need for barter.
- *Measure of value*. It enables a value to be placed on products so they can be bought and sold with ease. Money creates a unit of measure that enables comparisons between the relative values of products.
- *Store of value*. It is a convenient way of storing wealth so that it can be spent at a later date. Money will tend to hold its value in the short term as long as inflation remains low.

■ *Method of deferred payment.* It enables borrowing and lending. This means someone can borrow money in order to buy a product rather than waiting until enough funds have been saved. A price is usually set for borrowing and lending — this is known as the rate of interest.

Free market, mixed and command economies

An economy organises its resources in different ways to produce goods and services. This ranges along a continuum from a free market economy through to a mixed economy and then a centrally planned economy. Figure 3 shows the notion of a continuum.

Figure 3 Types of economic system

In reality, the vast majority of economies comprise a mixture of both private enterprise (the private sector) and state intervention (the public sector), thus being mixed economies. In the UK around 60% of resources are allocated by the private sector and 40% by the public sector. The government is a major provider of education, healthcare, defence and law and order in society. In other European economies (e.g. France, Germany and Sweden), the size of the public sector is greater, while in North America (the USA and Canada) it is lower. In all cases these are considered to be mixed economies.

A free market economy

A **free market economy** is where decisions on what, how and for whom to produce are left to the operation of the price mechanism. It is associated with the writings of the economists Adam Smith and Friedrich Hayek. Resources are privately owned and economic decision making is decentralised among many individual consumers and producers. There is minimum government intervention.

There are no pure free market economies in the world today since, in every economy, the government directly controls some resources and output. However, the proportion of government intervention tends to be significantly less in some developing countries, such as Malaysia and Thailand, compared to the developed world. Perhaps the best example of a developed country with a relatively small government sector is Japan.

Advantages of a free market economy
■ Economic efficiency and lower prices: competition means that firms try to keep production costs down in order to sell goods and services at competitive prices (productive efficiency). Competition also means that firms try to produce goods

Free market economy
Where all resources are privately owned and allocated via the price mechanism. There is minimal government intervention.

and services that consumers demand (allocative efficiency). This means the price mechanism will equate consumer demand with producer supply.

■ Quality of products: competition means firms continuously try to improve the quality of their products to gain an advantage over rivals. There is considerable consumer sovereignty: that is, consumer power in the market.

■ Greater choice: consumers can often choose to buy from a wide selection of goods and services; workers often have a wide choice of employment opportunities.

■ Financial incentives: entrepreneurs have an incentive to invest and take risks in order to earn profit; labour has an incentive to work hard to gain more earnings.

Disadvantages of a free market economy

■ Monopolies may form as a result of competition in some markets; rival firms get taken over or go out of business.

■ The distribution of income and wealth is very unequal and the lack of welfare support may lead to people living in absolute poverty.

■ External costs and benefits from production or consumption are sometimes ignored. For example, the price mechanism ignores the external costs of pollution and the external benefits of education.

■ Information gaps persist: people may consume excessive amounts of demerit goods such as drugs, tobacco and alcohol, unaware of their dangers. There is a lack of regulations and taxation to protect consumers.

■ An insufficient quantity of public goods and merit goods is provided in a market economy. Public goods include defence and street lighting, while merit goods include healthcare and education.

■ Erratic swings in the business cycle may cause high inflation during an economic boom and high unemployment during an economic slump.

A command economy

This is an economy where the government makes the decisions on what, how and for whom to produce. It is associated with the writings of Karl Marx, a nineteenth-century economist and philosopher who believed that production should be directed on the basis of human need rather than profit. In a **command economy**, the government has control of resources and economic decision making is centralised. There is no role for the price mechanism. Command economies can work effectively during times of national crisis: for example, the UK was run like one during the Second World War with great success. However, personal freedom and living standards tend to be jeopardised in such economic systems. One example today is North Korea.

Command economy
Where there is public ownership of resources and these are allocated by the government.

Advantages of a command economy

■ Cooperation between firms can lead to high levels of output. In general, the maximisation of output replaces the maximisation of profits as the key aim of firms.

■ There is a reduction in inequality compared to free market economies, since the government controls the wages of all workers.

■ The government may limit the external costs from production and consumption: for example, it can limit pollution emissions from firms and place severe taxes on harmful products such as tobacco and alcohol.

- The government can fund the provision of public goods such as defence and law and order; it can also increase the provision of goods which yield high external benefits to society, such as education and healthcare.
- The government has more control of the economy and so there are smaller swings in the business cycle, leading to less unemployment and inflation.

Disadvantages of a command economy

- The price mechanism is unable to operate and so markets may suffer from shortages (excess demand) and surpluses (excess supply), leading to an inefficient allocation of resources.
- The lack of competition between firms leads to inefficiency, and so productivity is low.
- The lack of competition leads to poor-quality products, especially when the emphasis is on maximising output rather than profit.
- There is less choice of goods and services for consumers to select from; labour may also be directed into specific jobs with no choice depending on their location.
- A lack of financial incentives: managers have no profit incentive to take risks by developing new goods and services, as the focus is on maximising output; labour has little incentive to work hard, since wages are fixed by the government.
- Under-performance of command economies: economic growth and living standards tend to grow at a much slower rate than in market-based economies. This was a major cause of the collapse of the Soviet Union during the early 1990s.

> **Exam tip**
>
> Note that the advantages of a command economy tend to represent disadvantages of a free market economy; similarly, the disadvantages of a command economy often represent advantages of a free market economy.

A mixed economy

This is an economy where decisions on what, how and for whom to produce are made partly by the private sector and partly by the government. Most developed countries in the world today fall under this classification. Examples are the UK, France, Germany, Canada, Australia and Sweden.

The rationale of a **mixed economy** is to gain the advantages of the market economy while avoiding its disadvantages through government intervention. It is associated with the writings of John Maynard Keynes in the early twentieth century. Often government intervention occurs to correct market failure: for example, the under-provision of merit goods such as education and healthcare or the non-provision of public goods such as defence. Government intervention usually arises to help markets work more effectively.

> **Knowledge check 6**
>
> Which type of economic system best describes the UK?

> **Mixed economy** Where some resources are owned and allocated by the private sector and some by the public sector.

Content Guidance

Summary

- Economics is concerned with how resources are allocated to provide for human wants. As resources are finite, there is an opportunity cost in producing a good or service, since the resources could have been used to produce alternative goods or services.
- Positive economic statements are facts which can be tested as true or false, whereas normative economic statements are value judgements which cannot be tested as true or false.
- The production possibility frontier illustrates the concepts of finite resources and opportunity cost. It can also be used to show unemployment and economic growth.
- Specialisation and the division of labour have led to huge increases in productivity.
- Money is anything that is generally acceptable in the payment of goods and services, or of debts. It has four functions: a medium of exchange, a measure of value, a store of value and a method of deferred payment.
- Most economies are mixed economies, where resources are allocated partly by private enterprise and partly by the government.

How markets work

Rational decision making in the market

There are many types of **market** — for example, clothing, motor vehicles and housing markets. One thing they have in common is that buyers and sellers come into contact for the purpose of exchange. A price is agreed for exchange to take place. By price, we mean the exchange value of a good or service. Buyers or consumers represent the 'demand' side of the market and sellers or producers represent the 'supply' side of the market.

Consumers are assumed to make rational decisions. This means consumers will allocate their income to maximise their utility or satisfaction from the goods and services they purchase. **Utility** refers to the amount of satisfaction obtained from consuming a good or service. Economists often make the assumption that utility can be measured.

Consumers do not have enough income to buy all the goods and services they want. Consequently, they have to make a choice about what goods and services to buy and in what quantities. A rational consumer will allocate his or her spending to maximise utility from the goods and services purchased. This requires the individual to equate the utility gained per £ spent on the last unit of each good or service. For example, if a consumer has an extra £100 to spend then it could be used to buy a £20 T-shirt and an £80 pair of shoes. We assume the T-shirt would provide 40 units of extra utility (or marginal utility) and the pair of shoes 160 units of extra utility (or marginal utility). In this way, the utility gained from the last unit of each good is equated (2 units of utility per £1 spent). Maximising consumer utility is shown by the following formula:

$$\frac{\text{Marginal utility of T-shirt}}{\text{Price of T-shirt}} = \frac{\text{Marginal utility of pair of shoes}}{\text{Price of pair of shoes}}$$

Producers are also assumed to make **rational decisions**. This means firms will use their resources to maximise profits from the goods and services produced. This involves producing at the level of output where total revenue exceeds total cost by the largest amount.

Demand

The buyers or consumers in a market are said to demand goods or services. **Demand** refers to the quantity of a good or service purchased at a given price over a given time period. Demand is different from just wanting a good or service. It is a want backed up by the ability to pay, which is also known as effective demand.

Movement along a demand curve

A **demand curve** shows the quantity of a good or service that would be bought over a range of different price levels in a given period of time. The demand curve for a good slope downwards from left to right because, as price falls, the good becomes cheaper compared to substitute goods and also more can be purchased with a given level of income.

Market Where consumers and producers come into contact with each other to exchange goods and services.

Utility The amount of satisfaction obtained from consuming a good or service.

Rational decision making Where consumers allocate their expenditure on goods and services to maximise utility, and producers allocate their resources to maximise profits.

Demand The quantity of a good or service purchased at a given price over a given time period.

Demand curve Shows the quantity of a good or service that would be bought over a range of different price levels in a given period of time.

The market demand curve is the horizontal summation of each individual demand curve for a particular good or service.

There is a movement along a demand curve for a good *only* when there is a change in its price. A fall in price causes an extension in demand, and a rise in price causes a contraction in demand, as shown in Figure 4.

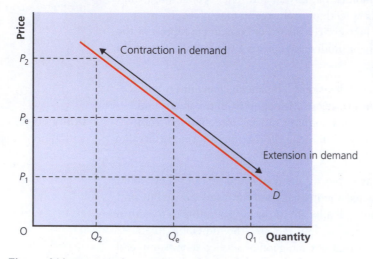

Figure 4 Movement along a demand curve

Marginal utility and the downward-sloping demand curve

The downward-sloping demand curve can also be explained by the concept of diminishing **marginal utility**. As one consumes more of a good, the utility or satisfaction gained from each extra unit will tend to fall or diminish. For example, at breakfast, the first bowl of cornflakes might give a high level of utility if one is hungry. However, a second bowl will not provide as much utility as the first, since one is less hungry. A third bowl of cornflakes will provide even less utility than the second bowl as one becomes full. This is an example of the law of **diminishing marginal utility**.

Note that total utility from consuming the bowls of cornflakes will increase as more is consumed, but this occurs at a diminishing rate. Eventually, one might feel sick from eating too many cornflakes and so marginal utility could fall drastically.

As marginal utility falls from each extra good consumed, it means consumers will only buy more of it if the price falls — hence the downward-sloping demand curve. Figure 5 shows the relationship between marginal utility, total utility and the amount of a good consumed.

Marginal utility The utility or satisfaction obtained from consuming one extra unit of a good or service.

Diminishing marginal utility As successive units of a good are consumed, the utility gained from each extra unit will fall.

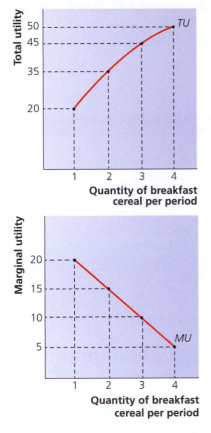

Figure 5 Total utility, marginal utility and the amount of a good consumed

Knowledge check 7

Why does the demand curve slope downwards from left to right?

Knowledge check 8

What causes a movement along a demand curve for a good?

Shifts in the demand curve

An increase in demand refers to the whole demand curve shifting outwards to the right at every price level. A decrease in demand refers to the whole demand curve shifting inwards to the left at every price level.

There are various factors which can shift the demand curve for a good. For example, the demand for Sony PlayStation 4 games consoles might increase due to:

- a fall in the price of complementary goods, such as computer games (Grand Theft Auto and FIFA Soccer)
- a rise in the price of substitute goods, such as the Microsoft Xbox One or the Nintendo Wii games consoles
- a change in fashion and tastes which makes games consoles more popular as a leisure activity among young people
- increased advertising of PlayStation games and consoles
- an increase in real incomes (for normal goods), meaning that the PlayStation becomes more affordable for people to buy
- a decrease in income tax, which leads to an increase in disposable income so that a PlayStation console becomes more affordable

- an increase in the population or a change in the age structure of the population so that there are more teenagers likely to purchase a PlayStation games console
- an increase in credit facilities, which makes it easier to obtain funds to pay for a PlayStation games console

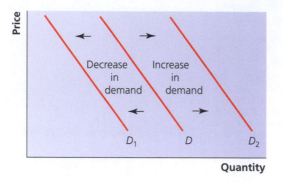

Figure 6 Shifts in demand curves

Figure 6 shows a decrease in demand by the shift of the demand curve leftwards to D_1 and an increase in demand is demonstrated by a rightward shift to D_2.

Price, income and cross elasticity of demand

Price elasticity of demand

Price elasticity of demand (*PED*) is the responsiveness in the demand for a good due to a change in its price. The formula to calculate it is:

$$PED = \frac{\text{percentage change in quantity demanded of good A}}{\text{percentage change in price of good A}}$$

In most circumstances, a minus answer is obtained, indicating that the two variables of price and demand move in opposite directions. There is a negative gradient.

Types of price elasticity of demand

If *PED* is greater than 1, the good is relatively price elastic: that is, the percentage change in demand is greater that the percentage change in price. For example, a 10% rise in the price of holidays to Florida may cause a 20% decrease in the quantity demanded; *PED* is −2.

If *PED* is less than 1, the good is relatively price inelastic: that is, the percentage change in demand is less than the percentage change in price. For example, a 10% fall in price of coffee may cause a 5% increase in the quantity demanded; *PED* is −0.5.

If *PED* is equal to 1, the good has unit elasticity: that is, the percentage change in demand is the same as the percentage change in price. For example, a 10% fall in the price of apples may cause a 10% rise in the quantity demanded; *PED* is −1.

If *PED* is equal to zero, the good is perfectly inelastic: that is, a change in price has no effect on the quantity demanded. The demand curve is vertical. An example might be heroin to a drug addict.

Exam tip

A change in price of a good will lead to a movement along the demand curve for that particular good; it will not shift the demand curve.

Knowledge check 9

What causes a shift in the demand curve for a good?

Price elasticity of demand The responsiveness of demand for a good or service to a change in its price.

Exam tip

Make sure you can calculate percentages and percentage change from data, since there are usually calculation questions on the exam papers.

Knowledge check 10

What does the minus sign mean in price elasticity of demand answers?

If *PED* is infinite, the good is perfectly elastic: that is, a rise in price causes demand to fall to zero. The demand curve is horizontal.

The demand curves in Figure 7 show the different elasticities.

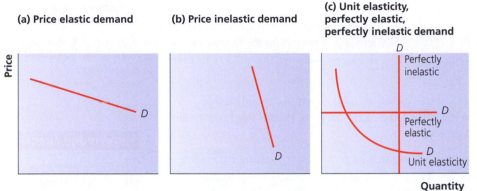

Figure 7 Different price elasticities of demand

The relationship between price elasticity of demand and total revenue

Elasticity varies along a straight-line demand curve, as shown in Figure 8. Elasticity falls as you move along the curve from the top left to the bottom right. At the mid-point, demand has unit elasticity.

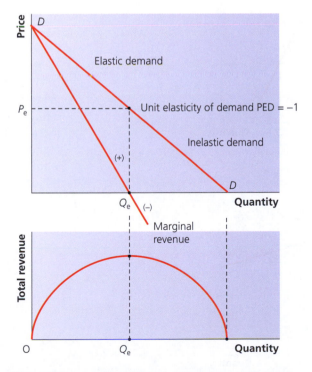

Figure 8 The relationship between price elasticity of demand and total revenue

Knowledge check 11

What does the actual figure represent in price elasticity of demand answers?

Exam tip

Do not confuse elasticity with the gradient of a demand curve. Straight-line demand curves have constant gradients but different elasticities along them.

Total revenue

Total revenue refers to the total payments a firm receives from selling a given quantity of goods or services. It is the price per unit of a good multiplied by the quantity sold. The total revenue a firm receives from selling a good will be equal to the total spending by consumers on that good.

A firm's total revenue will increase as long as price is moving towards the mid-position of the demand curve (where there is unit elasticity). It is important for firms to know the *PED* of their output when making pricing decisions, because this affects revenue and profitability.

If demand is elastic, then a cut in price increases total consumer spending and hence revenue to the firm. On the other hand, a rise in price causes total consumer spending to fall and so firms lose revenue.

If demand is inelastic, then an increase in price increases total consumer spending and hence revenue to the firm. On the other hand, a fall in price causes total consumer spending to fall and so firms lose revenue.

Once unit price elasticity has been reached, the firm is maximising its total revenue. Note the relationship between *PED* and marginal revenue, which falls during a move down the demand curve. As long as marginal revenue is positive, demand is price elastic. When marginal revenue is zero, demand is unit elastic; when marginal revenue is negative, demand is inelastic.

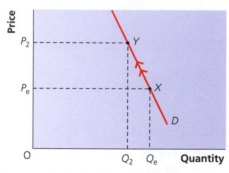

Figure 9 A rise in price increases total revenue under inelastic demand

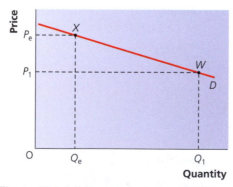

Figure 10 A fall in price increases total revenue under elastic demand

Total revenue The price per unit of a good multiplied by the quantity sold.

Knowledge check 12

Why might price elasticity of demand be useful to firms?

Knowledge check 13

Why might price elasticity of demand be useful to the government?

Exam tip

Be prepared to draw a diagram to show how a change in price will affect total revenue. For example, a rise in price will increase total revenue from OP_eXQ_e to OP_2YQ_2 when demand is inelastic (Figure 9); a fall in price will increase total revenue from OP_eXQ_e to OP_1WQ_1 when demand is elastic (Figure 10).

Determinants of price elasticity of demand

- *Availability of substitutes.* The more narrowly a good is defined, the more substitutes it tends to have and so its demand is elastic. For example, cod, a type of fish, has many substitutes such as plaice, rock, salmon and haddock. However, the more broadly a good is defined, the fewer substitutes it tends to have and so its demand is less elastic. For example, there are few close substitutes for fish as a whole and so demand tends to be relatively less elastic.
- *Luxury and necessity goods.* Luxury goods, such as racing cars and caviar, tend to have an elastic demand, whereas necessity goods, like bread and underwear, tend to have an inelastic demand.
- *Proportion of income spent on the good.* If a high percentage of income is spent on the good, as with a new car or boat, demand tends to be price elastic. However, for goods that take up a small percentage of income, such as newspapers and tomato sauce, demand will tend to be price inelastic.
- *Addictive and habit-forming goods.* Tobacco, alcohol and coffee are types of goods that tend to be price inelastic in demand.
- *The time period.* For most goods, demand is less elastic in the short run than in the long run. For example, a rise in the price of household electricity is likely to have only a minor effect on consumption in the short run. In the long run, households can cut back on consumption by switching to gas for their cooking and heating. This means demand eventually becomes more responsive to changes in price.
- *Brand image.* Some goods have a strong brand image — for example, Levi jeans and Coca Cola. Demand for these goods is typically price inelastic as consumers are often willing to pay a premium price for them.

Income elasticity of demand

Income elasticity of demand (YED) is the responsiveness of demand for a good or service to a change in real income. (Real income refers to the spending power of money income — the amount of goods and services which can be purchased with one's nominal income.) The formula to calculate YED is:

$$YED = \frac{\text{percentage change in demand for a good}}{\text{percentage change in real income}}$$

Normal goods

In most circumstances YED is positive, which means the two variables of income and demand move in the same direction. In other words, a rise in income causes a rise in quantity demanded. Note that some economists identify goods which have a YED above +1 as luxury goods. These are still a type of **normal good**.

A good with a YED less than 1 is relatively income inelastic and one with a YED above 1 is relatively income elastic in demand. A YED of 1 means it has unitary elasticity.

Inferior goods

Occasionally, YED is negative which means the two variables of income and demand move in opposite directions. This is because people tend to demand higher-quality goods as their incomes rise, substituting them for lower-quality products. Figure 11

Income elasticity of demand The responsiveness of demand for a good or service to a change in income.

Exam tip

Always show your workings in elasticity calculations and be careful to place the decimal point correctly. Marks are usually awarded for the workings even if the final answer is incorrect.

Normal good A good with a positive income elasticity of demand. As income rises, so too does demand for the good.

shows the demand curve for an **inferior good** compared with that of a normal good in relation to income. Examples of inferior goods are minced meat and supermarkets' own value brands of food.

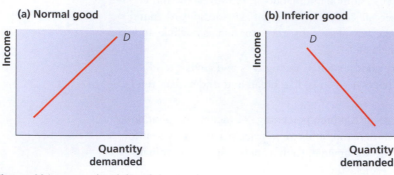

Figure 11 Income elasticity of demand

Cross elasticity of demand

Cross elasticity of demand (*XED*) is the responsiveness of demand for good B to a change in price of good A. The formula to calculate *XED* is:

$$XED = \frac{\text{percentage change in demand for good B}}{\text{percentage change in price of good A}}$$

> **Exam tip**
>
> A common mistake students make with cross elasticity of demand is to refer to the change in demand for one good affecting the change in demand for another good. This would lead to selection of the incorrect option in multiple-choice questions. Instead, it refers to how a change in price of one good affects the demand for another good.

Cross elasticity of demand is used to determine whether goods are complements or substitutes for each other.

Substitute goods

Substitute goods are in competitive demand. For example, a rise in the price of coffee may cause an increase in demand for tea. *XED* is positive for substitute goods, as the two variables of price and demand move in the same direction. There is a positive gradient.

Complementary goods

Complementary goods are in joint demand. They tend to be consumed together. For example, a fall in the price of tennis rackets may cause an increase in demand for tennis balls. *XED* is negative for complementary goods, as the two variables of price and demand move in opposite directions. There is a negative gradient.

Unrelated goods

Unrelated goods have an *XED* value of zero. For example, an increase in the price of cars will have no effect upon the demand for potatoes.

Inferior good A good with a negative income elasticity of demand. As income rises, demand for the good falls.

> **Exam tip**
>
> If there is a fall in demand or a fall in income, always show the minus signs in your calculations. It will increase your chances of gaining full marks.

> **Knowledge check 14**
>
> Distinguish between normal and inferior goods.

Cross elasticity of demand The responsiveness of demand for good B to a change in price of good A.

Figure 12 demonstrates cross elasticity of demand for complementary goods and substitute goods.

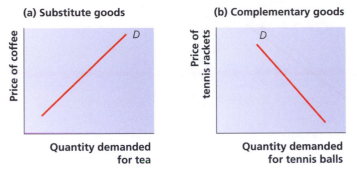

Figure 12 Cross elasticity of demand

Supply

The sellers or producers in a market are said to supply goods and services. **Supply** refers to the quantity of a good or service that firms are willing to sell at a given price and over a given period of time.

An upward-sloping supply curve

A **supply curve** is the quantity of a good or service that firms are willing to sell to a market over a range of different price levels in a given period of time. The supply curve slopes upwards from left to right since: as firms raise output in the short run, they face rising production costs and so pass these costs on to consumers by charging higher prices. Furthermore, as price rises, it encourages firms to supply more of a good to increase profits. Indeed, higher prices may encourage firms to enter a market and so raise supply.

The market supply curve is the horizontal summation of individual firms' supply curves for a particular good or service.

Movement along a supply curve

There is movement along a supply curve for a good *only* when there is a change in its price. A rise in price causes an extension in supply, and a fall in price causes a contraction in supply, as shown in Figure 13.

Shifts in the supply curve

An increase in supply refers to the whole supply curve shifting outwards to the right at every price level (to S_2 in Figure 14). A decrease in supply refers to the whole supply curve shifting inwards to the left at every price level (to S_1 in Figure 14).

There are various factors that can shift the supply curve of a good. For example, the supply of oil could increase due to:

- improvements in technology (e.g. the extraction of oil from more difficult places, such as under the sea bed in deeper water)
- a reduction in labour costs (e.g. lower wages for oil platform and oil refinery workers)

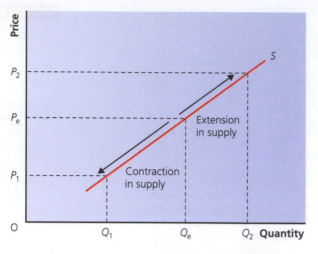

Figure 13 Movement along a supply curve

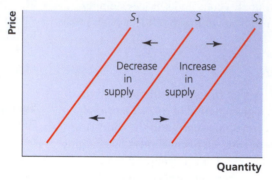

Figure 14 Shifts in the supply curve

- a reduction in capital costs (e.g. oil platforms, pipelines and refineries)
- a reduction in transport costs (e.g. an increase in the size of oil tankers)
- discovery of new oil fields (e.g. in the Falklands and Uganda)
- an increase in the number of firms in the oil industry
- a decrease in the market influences of OPEC (Organisation of Petroleum Exporting Countries), a producer cartel (this may occur if individual member states decide to produce more than the agreed oil quotas)
- good weather making it easier to extract oil from Alaska or under the sea bed
- a reduction in indirect taxation on oil
- an increase in government subsidies to oil producers

Price elasticity of supply

Price elasticity of supply (*PES*) is the responsiveness of the supply of a good to a change in its price. The formula to calculate *PES* is:

$$PES = \frac{\text{percentage change in supply of a good}}{\text{percentage change in price of a good}}$$

In most cases a positive answer is obtained, indicating that the two variables of price and quantity move in the same direction. There is a positive gradient.

If *PES* is greater than 1, the good is relatively price elastic: that is, the percentage change in supply is greater than the percentage change in price of the good.

If *PES* is less than 1, the good is relatively price inelastic: that is, the percentage change in supply is less than the percentage change in price of the good.

If *PES* is equal to 1, the good is unit elastic: that is, the percentage change in supply is the same as the percentage change in price of the good.

If *PES* is equal to zero, the good is perfectly inelastic: that is, a change in price has no effect on the quantity supplied. The supply curve is vertical.

If *PES* is infinite, the good is perfectly elastic. The supply curve is horizontal.

Figure 15 shows the different price elasticities of supply.

Knowledge check 19

What does a positive figure mean in price elasticity of supply answers?

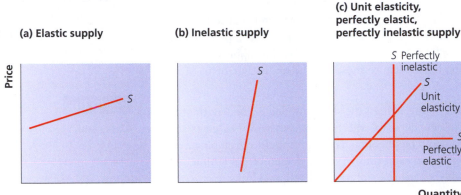

Figure 15 Different price elasticities of supply

Knowledge check 20

What does the 'number' represent in price elasticity of supply answers?

Determinants of price elasticity of supply

- *Level of spare capacity.* A high level of spare capacity in a firm means that it can raise production quickly, so supply tends to be elastic. A firm or industry operating at full capacity is unable to raise output quickly and so its supply tends to be inelastic.
- *State of the economy.* In a recession there are many unemployed resources and so there is a high level of spare capacity. Firms find it relatively easy to raise supply if needed.
- *Level of stocks of finished goods in a firm.* A high level of stocks means that the firm can increase supply quickly, so supply is elastic: for example, US motor vehicle manufacturers often have stockpiles of cars waiting to sell. Alternatively, a firm or industry operating with low stocks is unable to raise output quickly and so supply tends to be inelastic. This is more likely to be the case for a firm making designer wedding dresses.
- *Perishability of the product.* Some goods cannot be stockpiled: for example, some agricultural goods such as fresh fruit, vegetables and flowers are highly perishable.

These goods are typically inelastic in supply. On the other hand, manufactured goods tend to be non-perishable and so can be stockpiled by firms in order to meet anticipated increases in demand. Examples are household electrical goods such as fridges, freezers and washing machines.

■ *Ease of entry to an industry.* If there are high entry barriers to an industry then it will be difficult for new firms to enter, even with the attraction of high prices and profits. Sometimes existing producers deliberately create entry barriers, so supply may be restricted and inelastic.

■ *Time period under consideration.* This is perhaps the most important determinant of elasticity of supply. The short run is the period of time in which a firm is able to increase supply with its existing capacity. At least one factor input is likely to be fixed in quantity in the short run, which makes it difficult for a firm to raise production. Supply tends to be relatively inelastic. The long run is the period of time in which a firm is able to increase supply by adding to its production capacity. All factor inputs are variable in the long run, making it easier for a firm to raise production. Supply tends to be relatively elastic.

For many agricultural products, supply is inelastic in the short run because the output from the summer and autumn harvests depends on the amount of seed planted at the start of the year. It takes an even longer period of time to raise the supply of products from livestock, such as milk and beef, because these depend on the nurturing of animals over several years.

The supply of minerals may also be inelastic in the short run due to the length of time required to explore and discover new deposits and then extract them. The costs and technical complexities involved could be phenomenal. For example, developing a new iron ore mine in Western Australia, to cater for increasing demand from China, will require heavy machinery and the construction of new rail and road links.

Exam tip

Be careful not to confuse the determinants of price elasticity of supply with those of price elasticity of demand. This is one of the most common mistakes that examiners encounter when marking elasticity of supply questions.

Knowledge check 21

How might the price elasticity of supply for a good change over time?

Exam tip

Be prepared to draw a diagram to show how price elasticity of supply may vary over time to support your answer (see Figure 16). Usually 1 mark is available for this.

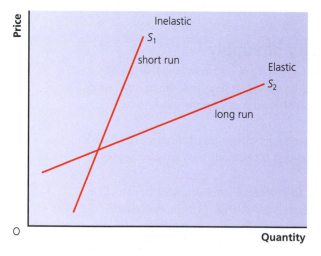

Figure 16 Elasticity of supply

Summary

- Economists assume that consumers and producers make rational decisions: this means consumers spend their income to maximise utility and producers allocate their resources to maximise profits.
- A movement along a demand curve is caused by a change in the price of the good, whereas a shift in a demand curve is caused by changes in real income, tastes, and the price of substitutes and complementary goods.
- The downward-sloping demand curve can be explained by diminishing marginal utility. As additional units of a good are consumed, marginal utility falls, so consumers will only buy more of a product as its price falls.
- A change in the price of a good towards unitary elasticity of demand will lead to an increase in total revenue.
- The determinants of price elasticity of demand for a good include the availability of substitutes, the proportion of income spent on it, the time period and whether it is addictive.

- Normal goods have a positive and inferior goods a negative income elasticity of demand.
- Substitute goods have a positive and complementary goods a negative cross elasticity of demand.
- A movement along a supply curve is caused by a change in the price of the good, whereas shifts in a supply curve are caused by other factors: for example, changes in costs of production, technology, the ability of firms to enter and exit an industry, indirect taxes and government subsidies.
- The determinants of price elasticity of supply of a good include the level of spare capacity, state of the economy, level of stocks, perishability, ease of entry and exit to an industry, and time period under consideration.
- A vertical supply curve indicates that supply of a good is perfectly price inelastic: for example, the capacity of Wembley stadium is 90,000 seats.

Price determination

Price is determined through the interaction of demand and supply in a competitive market. An **equilibrium price** and quantity occurs when there is a balance in the market. There is no tendency for price or quantity to change. The equilibrium price and quantity of a good are obtained from the point of intersection between the demand and supply curves. In the table below and Figure 17, the equilibrium price is £80 per unit and the quantity is 30 units per week.

Equilibrium price
The price where the quantity demanded equals the quantity supplied for a good or service in a market.

Price (£)	Quantity demanded per week	Quantity supplied per week
100	10	50
90	20	40
80	30	30
70	40	20
60	50	10

Excess supply and excess demand

In a free market, price cannot remain above or below the equilibrium position for long. For example, at a price of £100 there is an **excess supply** of 40 units. In order to sell the surplus, producers tend to reduce price and this encourages consumers to buy more. Demand extends and supply contracts until the equilibrium price of £80 is reached.

Excess supply Where the quantity supplied exceeds the quantity demanded for a good at the current market price.

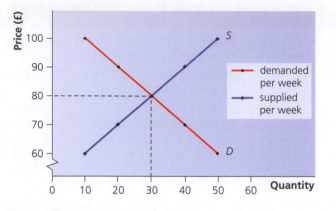

Figure 17 Market equilibrium

Knowledge check 22

What is likely to happen to price of a good if supply exceeds demand in a free market?

Excess demand Where the quantity demand exceeds the quantity supply for a good at the current market price.

Knowledge check 23

What is likely to happen to the price of a good if demand exceeds supply in a free market?

At a price of £60 there is an **excess demand** of 40 units. Consumers tend to bid up the price in order to obtain the good and this encourages producers to supply more. Supply extends and demand contracts until the equilibrium price of £80 is reached. Thus, the price mechanism automatically eliminates surpluses and shortages of a good — something that the economist Adam Smith referred to as the 'invisible hand' of the market.

Functions of the price mechanism

Price is the exchange value of a good or service. The **price mechanism** refers to the way price responds to changes in demand or supply for a product or factor input, so that a new equilibrium position is reached in a market. It is the principal method of allocating resources in a market economy. The price mechanism has several functions:

- *A rationing device.* Resources are scarce, which means that the goods and services produced from them are limited in supply. The price mechanism allocates these goods and services to those who are prepared to pay the most for them. In effect, price will rise or fall until equilibrium is reached between the quantity demanded and quantity supplied.
- *An incentive device.* Rising prices tend to act as an incentive to firms to produce more of a good or service, since higher profits can be earned. Rising prices also mean firms are able to cover the extra costs involved with increasing output.
- *A signalling device.* The price mechanism indicates changes in the conditions of demand or supply. For example, an increase in demand for a good or service raises its price and encourages firms to expand their supply, while a decrease in demand lowers the price and causes firms to contract their supply. Consequently, more or fewer resources are allocated to the production of a particular good or service.

Any of the factors which may shift demand or supply curves will lead to a change in price of a good or service.

Price mechanism The use of market forces to allocate resources in order to solve the economic problem of what, how and for whom to produce.

Exam tip

The most effective way to explain the functions of the price mechanism is by using a demand and supply diagram. For example, an increase in demand for gold will raise its price and offer a profit incentive for more to be supplied to the market. The rise in price also acts as a signal to the market for more to be produced.

Consumer and producer surplus

Consumer surplus is the extra amount of money consumers are prepared to pay for a good or service above what they actually pay. It is the utility or satisfaction gained from a good or service in excess of the amount paid for it.

Producer surplus is the extra amount of money paid to producers above what they are willing to accept to supply a good or service. It is the extra earnings obtained by a producer above the minimum required for them to supply the good or service.

The areas of consumer and producer surplus are shown in Figure 18. Consumer surplus is the area above the equilibrium price but below the demand curve; producer surplus is the area below the equilibrium price and above the supply curve.

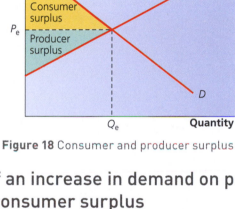

Figure 18 Consumer and producer surplus

The impact of an increase in demand on producer surplus and consumer surplus

An increase in demand for a good is likely to raise producer surplus and consumer surplus (assuming all other things remain equal). In Figure 19, demand increases from D to D_1, causing equilibrium price to rise from P_e to P_1. Producer surplus increases from BXP_e to BYP_1. The actual rise in producer surplus is area P_eXYP_1. Consumer surplus will also increase from area AXP_e to VYP_1.

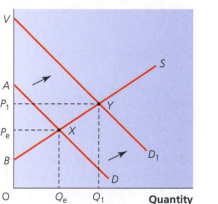

Figure 19 Impact of an increase in demand on consumer surplus and producer surplus

Knowledge check 24

Briefly explain how a decrease in demand for a good affects producer surplus and consumer surplus.

Exam tip

Do not assume that a fall in the price of a good will automatically increase consumer surplus. It depends on the reason for the fall in price. For example, a decrease in the demand for a good will lead to a lower price and lower consumer surplus.

The impact of a decrease in supply on consumer surplus and producer surplus

A decrease in supply of a good is likely to reduce consumer surplus and producer surplus. In Figure 20, supply decreases from S to S_1, causing equilibrium price to rise from P_e to P_1. Consumer surplus decreases from area AXP_e to AWP_1. The actual loss in consumer surplus is area WXP_eP_1. Producer surplus will also decrease from area BXP_e to GWP_1.

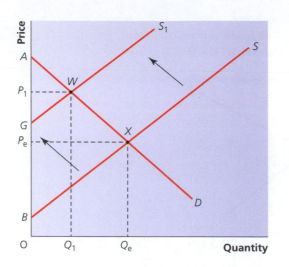

Figure 20 Impact of a decrease in supply on consumer surplus and producer surplus

Indirect taxes

A tax is a compulsory charge made by the government, on goods, services, incomes or capital. The purpose is to raise funds to pay for government spending programmes. There are two types of tax: direct and indirect.

A direct tax is levied directly on an individual or organisation. Direct taxes are generally paid on incomes: for example, personal income tax and corporation tax (on company profits).

An **indirect tax** is usually levied on the purchase of goods and services. It represents a tax on expenditure. There are two types of indirect tax: specific and *ad valorem* taxes. A specific tax is charged as a fixed amount per unit of a good, such as a litre of wine or a packet of cigarettes. An excise tax is a good example. An *ad valorem* tax is charged as a percentage of the price of a good: for example, VAT of 20% is added on to restaurant meals.

The imposition of an indirect tax raises the price of a good or service. The tax is added to the supply price, effectively causing the supply curve to shift vertically upwards and to the left (a decrease in supply). A specific tax causes a parallel shift of the supply curve to the left, as shown in part (a) of Figure 21. An *ad valorem* tax causes a pivotal rotation of the supply curve to the left, as shown in part (b).

Knowledge check 25

Briefly explain how a decrease in supply of a good affects consumer surplus and producer surplus.

Exam tip

Do not assume that a rise in the price of a good will automatically increase producer surplus. It depends on the reason for the rise in price. For example, a decrease in the supply of a good will lead to a rise in price but a lower producer surplus.

Exam tip

For multiple-choice and short-answer questions on consumer surplus or producer surplus, where a diagram is provided, you should always state the original area, the new area and the actual increase or decrease in area. This could be done by annotating the diagram.

Indirect tax A tax imposed on goods or services supplied by businesses. It includes both specific and *ad valorem* taxes.

Knowledge check 26

Distinguish between a specific tax and an *ad valorem* tax.

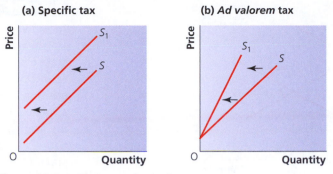

Figure 21 Specific tax and *ad valorem* tax

The incidence of an indirect tax

The **incidence of a tax** usually falls partly on consumers and partly on producers, depending on the relative price elasticities of demand and supply for the good or service. A combination of price inelastic demand and price elastic supply tends to place most of the tax burden on consumers; addictive goods such as tobacco and alcohol tend to be price inelastic in demand. This means that firms are able to pass most of the burden of tax on to consumers via higher prices.

However, a combination of price elastic demand and price inelastic supply tends to place most of the tax burden on the producers. It may also lead to a significant reduction in output and employment. Consequently, a government may be reluctant to place high indirect taxes on these types of goods or services.

Figure 22 shows the effects of a specific tax on a good. Before the tax, equilibrium price is P_e and quantity Q_e. After the tax is imposed, the supply curve shifts to S_1 and the equilibrium price rises to P_1 while quantity falls to Q_1. The total tax area is $XYWP_1$.

The incidence of tax paid by consumers is shown by the actual rise in market price from P_e to P_1. Consumers pay the amount of tax shown by the area XZP_eP_1. The tax paid by producers is the remaining area $ZYWP_e$.

> **Exam tip**
>
> To show an indirect tax on a diagram, always start from the *new* equilibrium price position and then draw a vertical line down to the original supply curve. In Figure 22 the starting point is *X*, and the line is drawn down to *Y*. Many students make the mistake of starting from the original equilibrium price position (shown as *E*) and then end up with the wrong tax area.

Subsidies

A **subsidy** is a grant, usually provided by the government, to encourage suppliers to increase production of a good or service, leading to a fall in its price. Bus and train companies are often given subsidies in order to increase the number of bus and train services, which benefits both the firms and consumers.

Incidence of tax The distribution of the tax paid between consumers and producers.

> **Exam tip**
>
> One way of working out the part of an indirect tax paid by consumers is to consider the actual increase in market price of a good once the tax is imposed. The rise in market price is the part of the tax paid by consumers; the rest of the tax is then paid by producers.

Subsidy A government grant to firms, which reduces production costs and encourages an increase in output.

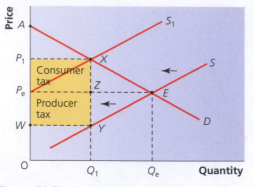

Figure 22 The incidence of taxation

A subsidy is often paid directly to producers, but as they respond by increasing output, the market price falls and this indirectly passes on some of the gain to consumers. If demand is price inelastic, then the market price falls by a relatively large amount, increasing the benefits to consumers. If demand is price elastic, then market price falls by a relatively small amount and so there is less gain for consumers. Figure 23 shows the imposition of a government subsidy for a good.

Before the subsidy, equilibrium price is P_e and Q_e. After the subsidy is imposed, the supply curve shifts to S_2 and equilibrium price falls to P_2 while the quantity rises to Q_2. The total subsidy area is $RLGP_2$.

The amount of subsidy that consumers gain is shown by the actual fall in market price from P_e to P_2. They gain by paying a lower price for the good. The consumer subsidy area is RTP_eP_2. The remaining subsidy area of $TLGP_e$ represents the gain made by producers.

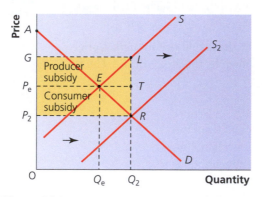

Figure 23 A government subsidy to producers

Alternative views of consumer behaviour

Economists often assume that consumers behave in a rational manner and so allocate their income to buy goods and services to maximise their utility or satisfaction. (Note that some income may also be saved for future use if the utility gained is greater than current spending on extra items.) Rational economic decision making comes from a deductive approach to the subject, where models are created on the basis of how consumers are *expected* to behave and that their aim *should* be to maximise total utility.

Exam tip

To show a subsidy on a diagram, always start from the *new* equilibrium price position and then draw a vertical line up to the original supply curve. In Figure 23 the starting point is R, and the line is drawn up to L. Many students make the mistake of starting from the original equilibrium price position (shown as E) and then end up with the wrong subsidy area.

Exam tip

One way of working out the part of a subsidy that is gained by consumers is to consider the actual fall in market price once the subsidy is applied. The fall in market price is the part of the subsidy from which consumers directly benefit; the rest of the subsidy remains with producers.

Knowledge check 27

How does a unit subsidy affect the market price and output for a good?

However, an inductive approach to economics starts by investigating how consumers *actually* behave and then develops models from the results. This alternative view of consumer behaviour attempts to explain why they may not always make rational economic decisions. Indeed, consumers may be considered irrational in seeking a *satisfactory* level of utility rather than *maximising* utility. There are several factors which help to explain this behaviour, and these are considered in the following sections.

Knowledge check 28

What is meant by alternative views of consumer behaviour?

The influence of other people's behaviour

Consumers are influenced by the behaviour of others: for example, if some people start buying a share in a particular company, others may follow, despite this causing the price to rise and making the share less of a bargain. This 'herd like' mentality is often displayed in various markets where it has become clear that consumers who come late to the market receive little benefit. Property markets offer a reminder of how consumers could lose out by purchasing at the peak of an economic cycle, only to see asset values crash in a downturn.

The importance of habitual behaviour

Consumers are creatures of habit and prefer what they know and have, rather than risking something new where there is more uncertainty: for example, switching bank accounts to get lower charges or switching energy supplier to get lower gas and electricity prices. This consumer inertia could also be explained by the difficulties involved in changing bank or energy supplier — there may be mistakes in the final bills and switchover, and considerable time may be wasted in filling out forms. It appears that for some consumers, doing nothing is preferred to obtaining better deals.

Furthermore, consumers are often unrealistic about their future behaviour. For example, many adults are overweight and yet continue their habit of eating too much. This is because they expect to change their habit and eat less in the near future. However, often they do not eat less and so remain overweight, leading to long-term health problems. This is a case of overvaluing the utility from eating too much today and undervaluing the utility of being thinner and having fewer health problems in the future.

Consumer weakness at computation

Many consumers have difficulty in calculating the best buys: for example, when shopping at a supermarket and facing a choice of different-sized packs of the same good — the larger size is not always the cheapest per unit. Consumers may simply lack the skills required to calculate the best buy.

Imperfect market knowledge underlies the weakness that some consumers display in computation. In reality, consumers do not always buy a good at the cheapest price possible or a good of the best quality, since markets do not always operate efficiently. It is impossible for consumers to have full market knowledge on which to base their decisions. This is a theme investigated further in the next section.

Knowledge check 29

Outline three reasons why consumers may not maximise total utility.

Content Guidance

Summary

- In a competitive market, the equilibrium price and quantity of a good or service is determined by the interaction of demand and supply.
- The price mechanism is the use of market forces to allocate resources in order to solve the economic problem of what, how and for whom to produce. Its three functions are to operate as a rationing, incentive and signalling device in the market.
- Consumer surplus is the utility or satisfaction gained from a good or service in excess of the price paid for it. Producer surplus is the extra earnings obtained by a producer above the minimum required for them to supply the good or service.
- An excess demand for a good will cause price to rise until equilibrium is reached; an excess supply of a good will cause price to fall until equilibrium is reached.
- An indirect tax on a good will cause an inward shift in the supply curve, leading to a fall in output and a rise in price.
- A unit subsidy on a good will cause an outward shift in the supply curve, leading to a rise in output and a fall in price.
- Alternative views of consumer behaviour are based on real-world investigations of how consumers actually behave. This indicates that consumers may not aim to maximise total utility, or they may be confused over the behaviour required to do this.

Market failure

Types of market failure

Market failure occurs when the price mechanism causes an inefficient allocation of resources and so leads to a net welfare loss. Consequently, resources are not allocated to their best or optimum use.

There are various types of market failure and you may come across different classifications in your textbooks. However, Theme 1 of the specification focuses on the following: externalities, under-provision of public goods and information gaps. Each of these is now considered in turn.

Externalities

Externalities are those costs or benefits which are external to an exchange. They are third-party effects ignored by the price mechanism.

Externalities are also known as *indirect costs* and *benefits*, or as *spillovers from production* or *consumption* of a good or service. In effect, external costs are *negative externalities* and external benefits are *positive externalities*.

External costs

External costs may occur in the production and the consumption of a good or service. An example of an external cost in production is a chemical firm polluting a river with its waste. This causes an external cost to the fishing and water supply industries. Fish catches may be reduced and it may become very expensive to purify water to meet the European Commission's safety standards.

An example of an external cost in consumption is a person smoking tobacco, polluting the air for others. The effect is to cause passive smoking, where non-smokers may suffer the same illnesses as smokers.

Private costs

In a free market, producers are only concerned with the **private costs** of production. These are costs internal to the firm, which it pays for directly. These costs include wages for workers, rent of buildings, payment for raw materials, machinery costs, electricity and gas costs, insurance, packaging and transport costs from running lorries. Private costs may also refer to the market price that a consumer pays for a good or service.

Social costs

By adding private costs to external costs, we obtain **social costs**. This means that external costs are the difference between private costs and social costs. The marginal private cost and marginal social cost curves often diverge, indicating that external costs increase disproportionately with output. However, it is possible that external costs per unit of output remain constant, in which case the marginal private cost and marginal social cost curves are drawn parallel to each other. The relationship between private cost, external cost and social cost is shown in Figure 24.

Market failure When the price mechanism causes an inefficient allocation of resources, leading to a net welfare loss.

External costs Negative third-party effects outside of a market transaction.

Exam tip

When defining external costs, offer two ideas as there are often 2 marks available: for example, 'They are negative third-party effects and represent costs outside of the market transaction.' Also be prepared to give an example, such as pollution from coal extraction or gas fracking.

Private costs Costs internal to a market transaction, which are therefore taken into account by the price mechanism.

Social costs The sum of external costs and private costs from a market transaction.

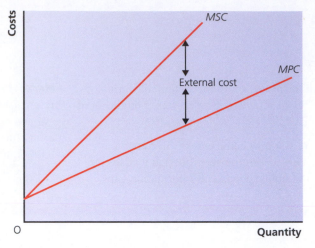

Figure 24 The relationship between private cost, external cost and social cost in the production of a good

Note that the Edexcel specification focuses on diagrammatic analysis of external costs in production.

External benefits

External benefits may occur in the production and consumption of a good or service. An example of an external benefit in production is the recycling of waste materials such as newspapers, glass and tins. It has the benefit of reducing the amount of waste disposal for landfill sites as well as re-using materials for production. It helps to promote sustainable economic growth.

An external benefit in consumption is the vaccination of an individual against various diseases. It reduces the possibility of other people catching a disease who come into contact with the vaccinated individual.

External benefits
Positive third-party effects outside of a market transaction.

> **Exam tip**
>
> When defining external benefits, offer two ideas as there are often 2 marks available: for example, 'They are positive third-party effects and represent benefits outside of the market transaction.' Also be prepared to give an example, such as increased house prices for homeowners near an urban regeneration scheme.

Private benefits

In a free market, consumers are only concerned with the **private benefits** or utility from consuming a good or service. Economists assume this can be measured by the price that consumers are prepared to pay for a good or service. Private benefits may also refer to the revenue that a firm obtains from selling a good or service.

Private benefits
Benefits internal to a market transaction, which are therefore taken into account by the price mechanism.

Social benefits

By adding private benefits to external benefits, we obtain **social benefits**. This means external benefits are the difference between private benefits and social benefits. The marginal private benefit and marginal social benefit curves often diverge, indicating that external benefits increase disproportionately with output consumed, as shown in Figure 25. However, it is possible that external benefit per unit consumed will remain constant, in which case the marginal private benefit and marginal social benefit curves are drawn parallel to each other.

Social benefits The sum of external benefits and private benefits from a market transaction.

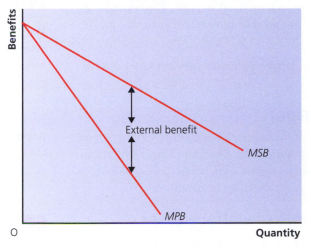

Figure 25 The private benefits, external benefits and social benefits from the consumption of a good

Knowledge check 31

What are social benefits?

Note that the Edexcel specification focuses on diagrammatic analysis of external benefits in consumption of goods and services.

Table 1 Examples of external costs and external benefits

	External costs	External benefits
Production	A waste disposal firm dumping toxic waste at sea, which destroys fish life.	A paper and glass recycling plant, which reduces the waste for landfill sites.
	Burning coal in power stations to create electricity, adding to global warming.	Construction of the London Crossrail project, increasing inward investment and raising local property prices.
	Increased production of biofuels, which destroy rain forests and increase food prices.	The use of wind turbines and tidal power to create electricity. These are renewable forms of energy, which emit less carbon emissions than fossil fuels.
Consumption	Excess alcohol intake, which leads to vandalism.	Education and training programmes, which increase human capital levels. Higher labour productivity increases profits for firms.
	Increased road congestion around the expansion of Heathrow airport.	Improving the quality of one's garden, which increases the value of neighbouring houses.
	Tobacco smoking, which affects passive smokers.	The consumption of vaccinations, which help reduce the spread of diseases and so increase life expectancy for millions.

The free market equilibrium

The supply curve for a firm is the marginal private cost curve (*MPC*). The addition of all the *MPC* curves of firms in a market for a particular good or service will form the market supply curve.

The demand curve for consumers is the marginal private benefit curve (*MPB*). Economists assume that it is possible to measure the benefit obtained from consuming a good by the price people are prepared to pay for it. As an individual consumes more units of a good, the marginal benefit (marginal utility) will fall. This is why the demand curve slopes downwards from left to right. The addition of all the consumers' *MPB* curves for a particular good or service will form the market demand curve.

Market equilibrium occurs at the price and output position where marginal private benefit equals marginal private cost.

The social optimum equilibrium

The **social optimum** equilibrium level of output or price for a good or service occurs where marginal social cost (*MSC*) equals marginal social benefit (*MSB*). The social cost of producing the last unit of output equals the social benefit from consuming it. When the social optimum is reached in a market, welfare is maximised.

External costs and the triangle of welfare loss

The free market ignores negative externalities. However, adding external costs on to the production of a good or service, such as the production of chemical goods, causes the supply curve of the firm to shift to the left and become the marginal social cost curve, shown in Figure 26.

Market equilibrium
Where marginal private benefit equals marginal private cost.

Social optimum Where marginal social benefit equals marginal social cost.

Knowledge check 32

Distinguish between the market equilibrium and social optimum positions in a market.

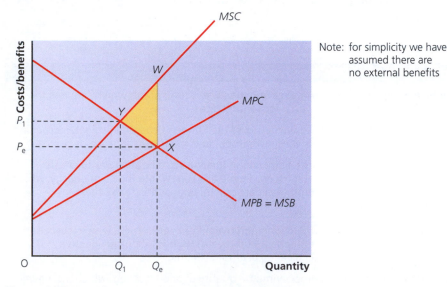

Figure 26 External costs and the triangle of welfare loss

Assuming there are no external benefits in the production of a chemical good, the social optimum equilibrium is at price OP_1 and quantity OQ_1. When external costs are ignored, there is underpricing and overproduction. There is an excess of social costs over social benefits for the marginal output between Q_e and Q_1.

The marginal social cost of the output slice Q_eQ_1 is Q_eWYQ_1, which exceeds the marginal social benefit of this output, Q_eXYQ_1. The excess of social costs over social benefits is shown by the triangle XWY. This is the area of welfare loss to society; the market has failed, since negative externalities are ignored.

External benefits and the triangle of welfare gain

The free market ignores positive externalities. However, adding external benefits on to the consumption of a good or service, such as the consumption of vaccinations, causes the demand curve to shift to the right and become the marginal social benefit curve, shown in Figure 27.

Assuming there are no external costs in the consumption of vaccinations in a free market, the social optimum equilibrium is at OP_2 and quantity OQ_2. When external benefits are ignored, there is underpricing and underproduction. There is an excess of social benefits over social costs for the marginal output between Q_e and Q_2. Thus, by raising output from OQ_e to OQ_2, welfare could be increased.

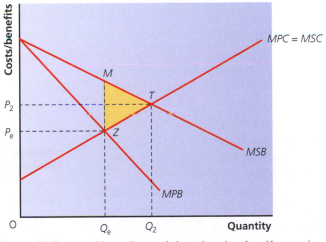

Figure 27 External benefits and the triangle of welfare gain

The marginal social benefit of the output slice Q_eQ_2 is Q_eMTQ_2, which exceeds the marginal social cost of this output, Q_eZTQ_2. The excess of social benefits over social costs is shown by the triangle MTZ. This is the area of welfare gain to society; the market has failed, since positive externalities are ignored.

The impact of external costs on consumers and producers

External costs can be ignored by consumers and producers when they make their economic decisions, so causing market failure. This leads to:

- Overproduction, since the free market level of output exceeds the social optimum level of output.
- Underpricing, since the free market price is below the social optimum price.
- Welfare loss, since marginal social costs exceed marginal social benefits.
- Concerns over the availability of resources for future generations. For example, overfishing will lead to a collapse in fish stocks, which may become unsustainable.
- Concerns over pollution levels. For example, burning fossil fuels to produce energy could lead to global warming and consequent problems of climate change. Air pollution could also increase respiratory diseases and reduce life expectancy.
- Calls for government intervention to internalise the external costs and so correct market failure. This may take the form of indirect taxes and trade pollution permits (refer to section on government intervention, page 46).

Knowledge check 35

Why do external costs cause market failure?

The impact of external benefits on consumers and producers

External benefits can be ignored by consumers and producers making their economic decisions and so cause market failure. This leads to:

- Underproduction since the free market level of output is less than the social optimum level of output.
- Underpricing since the free market price is below the social optimum price. (Note that society should be prepared to pay more for the goods or services to take account of external benefits.)
- Potential welfare gain, since marginal social benefits exceed marginal social costs.
- Concerns over the long-term implications of underproduction. For example, underprovision of education and healthcare could lead to lower economic growth and a less competitive economy. Living standards may rise more slowly.
- Calls for government intervention to internalise the external benefits and so correct market failure. This may take the form of regulation, government provision and subsidies (see the section 'Government intervention', page 47).

Knowledge check 36

Why do external benefits cause market failure?

Public goods

Some goods may not be produced at all through the markets, despite offering significant benefits to society. Where this occurs it is known as a 'missing market' and the goods are called **public goods**. These goods involve a large element of collective consumption: for example, national defence, flood defence systems, the criminal justice system and refuse collection.

Public goods Those goods that have non-rivalry and non-excludability in their consumption.

Public goods demonstrate characteristics of non-excludability and non-rivalry.

- Non-excludability means that once a good has been produced for the benefit of one person, it is impossible to stop others from benefiting.
- Non-rivalry means that as more people consume a good and enjoy its benefits, it does not reduce the amount available for others. In effect, it is non-diminishable.

Once a public good has been provided, the cost of supplying it to an extra consumer is zero. Further examples include public firework displays, lighthouses, public beaches, public parks, drains and street lighting.

Private goods

Private goods are the opposite of public goods. They display characteristics of rivalry and excludability in consumption. An example of a private good is a Mars bar, the consumption of which directly excludes other people from consuming that particular bar. The owners of private goods are able to use private property rights which prevent other people from consuming them. Private goods can also be rejected, which means one has a choice over whether to consume them or not.

The free-rider problem

In a free market economy, public goods are underprovided due to the free-rider problem. Once a public good has been provided for one individual, it is automatically provided for all. The market fails because it is not possible for firms to withhold the good from those consumers who refuse to pay for it. Examples are national defence and street pavements.

The rational consumer would wait for someone else to provide the good and then reap the rewards by consuming it for free. However, if everyone waits for others to supply a public good then it may never be provided. The non-excludability characteristic means that the price mechanism cannot develop as free riders will not pay. Firms are reluctant to supply such a good in a free market as it is difficult to gain profits from it. The solution is for government to provide public goods and fund them from general taxation.

> **Exam tip**
>
> Do not make the mistake of calling the National Health Service and state education examples of public goods. There is rivalry in the consumption of these goods. It is more appropriate to describe them as goods which yield external benefits, or merit goods.

Information gaps

Information gaps can lead to market failure due to either consumers or producers having more market knowledge than the other about a particular good or service. It means there is an unequal balance upon which to conduct economic transactions between them. A good example is the second-hand car market discussed later in this section.

Knowledge check 37

When might a public beach cease to be a public good?

Private goods Those goods that have rivalry and excludability in their consumption.

Knowledge check 38

What is meant by the free-rider problem?

Knowledge check 39

Why do public goods represent a type of market failure?

Information gaps Where consumers, producers or the government have insufficient knowledge to make rational economic decisions.

Information gaps can also lead to market failure when consumers or producers simply lack perfect knowledge about a particular good or service and so end up making non-rational economic decisions. A good example is the pension market, where people tend to make too few contributions for their retirement. This is also discussed later in this section.

Symmetric information

In competitive markets, it is often assumed that consumers and producers have **symmetric information** when making their economic decisions — that they have access to the same information about a good or service in a market. Assuming that consumers and producers act in a rational way, symmetric information will lead to an efficient allocation of resources. This means consumers will buy a good or service from a producer offering the best deal, taking into account things like price, quality, reliability and after-sales service.

Symmetric information
Where consumers and producers have access to the same information about a good or service in the market.

Asymmetric information

In reality, consumers and producers have **asymmetric information** — that is, unequal market knowledge upon which to make their economic decisions — and this could lead to a misallocation of resources.

Asymmetric information
Where consumers and producers have unequal access to information about a good or service in the market.

How imperfect market knowledge may lead to a misallocation of resources

Producer knowledge may exceed consumer knowledge. A second-hand car salesman, for example, may have greater knowledge of the history of vehicles for sale as well as more technical knowledge than consumers. This could lead to a consumer paying too much for a poor-quality car. The fear of buying a defective car tends to reduce the market price for all second-hand cars, even the good-quality ones. Consequently, the losers could be both buyers and sellers, depending on the car sold. This is known as a lemon market.

The solution is to have inspection schemes offered by motoring organisations such as the Automobile Association. It can inspect a car on behalf of consumers to overcome information failure.

Similar problems arise in the market for healthcare, where private doctors may end up over-treating patients in order to increase their profits. This has occurred in some cases of cosmetic surgery. The solution is to have a watchdog body such as the General Medical Council to investigate and prosecute offending practitioners.

In other cases, consumer knowledge may exceed producer knowledge. A consumer may purchase an insurance policy, concealing information about himself or simply knowing more than the insurance company about his intended future actions. This might include having a risky lifestyle. The insurance company may then provide insurance at too low a price or insure someone who might be too risky to insure, and therefore may make a loss. This could lead to insurers exiting the market or refusing to make the payouts due. The solution is to have a watchdog body with powers to investigate and prosecute fraudulent insurance claims.

Imperfect market knowledge means that many people fail to make sufficient contributions to their pension scheme (a scheme to provide an income to people when they retire from work). This reflects the uncertainty surrounding their long-term future circumstances, such as financial outgoings, quality of health and longevity. There is also risk associated with the type of pension scheme entered into, as returns are linked to the performance of the stock market. Given these problems, it is not surprising that many people make so little provision for retirement and end up in poverty in old age. The solution partly involves government intervention which makes it compulsory for workers to contribute to a National Insurance scheme that pays for state pensions.

Knowledge check 40

Why does imperfect market information lead to market failure?

Summary

- There are various forms of market failure: for example, externalities, underprovision of public goods and information gaps.
- External costs and benefits arise due to third-party effects in market transactions that the price mechanism ignores.
- External costs in production lead to a welfare loss triangle as the free market output equilibrium exceeds the social optimum position.
- External benefits in consumption lead to a potential welfare gain triangle as the free market output equilibrium is less than the social optimum position.
- Public goods display characteristics of non-rivalry and non-excludability in consumption.
- Public goods are underprovided or not provided at all in a free market economy due to the free-rider problem.
- Information gaps mean consumers and producers may make economic decisions on buying and selling goods which reduce their welfare. This can be seen in the underconsumption of healthcare, education and pensions, or the overconsumption of tobacco, alcohol and gambling.
- Symmetric information is where consumers and producers have equal access to market knowledge; asymmetric information is where consumers and producers have unequal access to market knowledge.

Government intervention

Government intervention in markets

The UK is mixed economy, which means both private enterprise and the government allocate resources to solve the economic problem of what, how and for whom to produce. Often the government intervenes where there is market failure and attempts to correct this so that resources are allocated more efficiently.

There are various measures a government could undertake to correct market failure: for example, indirect taxation, subsidies, maximum prices, minimum prices, trade pollution permits, regulation, provision of public goods and provision of market information. The relative merits of each form of intervention are now considered in relation to different types of market failure. Note that the disadvantages of these measures point to the possibility of government failure.

Knowledge check 41

What is the key reason for government intervention in markets?

Indirect taxation

Indirect taxes are taxes levied on the expenditure of goods or services. The government often imposes taxes on goods which have significant external costs, such as petrol, tobacco, alcohol and electricity generated from burning fossil fuels.

Figure 28 shows the market for petrol, including both the marginal private cost curve (MPC) and the marginal social cost curve (MSC). In a free market the equilibrium price is OP_e and the equilibrium quantity OQ_e. However, the social optimum price is OP_1 and the social optimum quantity OQ_1, where marginal social cost (MSC) equals marginal social benefit (MSB) for the last unit produced. The vertical distance ZY represents the external cost (air pollution) for each litre of petrol consumed.

By placing a tax equal to the external cost of ZY per litre, the government successfully internalises the pollution. The total tax collected is shown by the area P_1YZW. Both producers and consumers pay the tax, depending on the relative elasticities of demand and supply. The consumer tax area is YP_1P_eT and the producer tax area is P_eTZW.

Knowledge check 42

Why are there high indirect taxes on tobacco, alcohol and petrol?

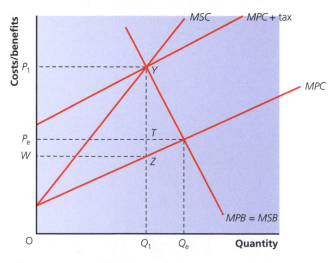

Figure 28 An indirect tax on petrol

Advantages of indirect taxes to correct market failure

- In the case of pollution, indirect taxes are based on the principle that the polluters (both producer and consumer) pay, helping to internalise the external costs.
- They work with market forces so that choice still exists in terms of consumption and production, unlike the effects of some regulations.
- The level of pollution should fall as output of the good or service is reduced and the price increased — the social optimum position of $MSB = MSC$ can be achieved.
- Tax funds are raised for the government and these can be used to clean up the environment or to compensate the victims of pollution.
- Indirect taxes are difficult to evade as they are often included in the market price. The sellers collect the tax revenue and send it to government.
- Indirect taxes are convenient, since they tend to be paid in small amounts and regularly rather than in one lump sum.

Disadvantages of indirect taxes to correct market failure

- It is difficult to quantify external costs and then place a monetary value on them. Consequently, the social optimum position might not be achieved.
- Indirect taxes increase the costs of production for firms, making them less competitive than firms in other countries where such taxes are not applied.
- Widespread use of indirect taxes may be inflationary.
- Firms may relocate to other countries with less stringent taxes on production.
- The demand for the good or service may be price inelastic and so the overall reduction in pollution levels may be small.
- The tax revenue raised may not be used to compensate victims or clean up the environment.
- In the case of some goods, unintended consequences may occur such as the development of illegal markets: for example, tobacco and alcohol smuggling to avoid high taxes.
- The regressive nature of indirect taxes leads to further unintended consequences: for example, the burden of payment tends to fall on low-income rather than high-income groups.

Exam tip

One evaluation technique is to consider the impact on different interest groups: for example, the economic effects of an increase in tax on petrol. This may have a bigger impact on consumers than on petrol producers, since demand is price inelastic. Petrol firms will be able to pass on most of the tax to consumers. The government is also likely to benefit from increased tax revenue.

Subsidies

A subsidy is a grant provided by the government to encourage the production and consumption of a particular good or service. Subsidies are often applied on goods or services with significant external benefits, such as education and healthcare. They may also be given to alternative forms of economic activity which create less pollution, such as public transport and renewable energy.

Figure 29(a) shows the application of a unit subsidy to the market for electricity from renewable energy sources. The effect of the subsidy is to lower the price of each kilowatt of electricity from P_e to P_1 and to increase the quantity from Q_e to Q_1.

The subsidy per unit is AB and the total subsidy area is $ABCP_1$. Part of the subsidy is passed on to consumers in the form of a lower price of electricity, equal to the area AGP_eP_1. The other portion of the subsidy ($GBCP_e$) remains with the producer. The lower price of electricity from renewable energy sources will help decrease the demand for electricity from non-renewable sources from D to D_1 (Figure 29(b)).

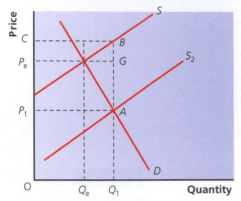
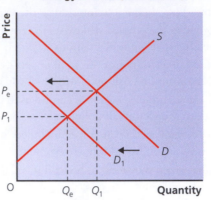

Figure 29 A unit subsidy for renewable electricity generation and the impact on the market for non-renewable electricity generation

Advantages of subsidies applied to renewable energy markets

- Subsidies can reduce air pollution and other forms of external costs.
- Subsidies on renewable energy generation promote sustained economic growth.
- The rate of consumption of non-renewable energy resources is reduced.
- Subsidies work with market forces. They help to internalise the external benefits from renewable forms of energy so that the social optimum level of output can be reached.

Disadvantages of subsidies applied to renewable energy markets

- It is difficult to quantify external benefits and then place a monetary value on them. Consequently, the social optimum position might not be achieved.
- There is an opportunity cost to government subsidies. They may lead to higher taxes or cuts in government spending elsewhere. They may be a waste of money: for example, many subsidised bus services operate along routes with hardly any passengers.
- Unintended consequences may occur: for example, firms may become dependent on the subsidies and inefficient in production.
- Wind power and solar power may be less reliable sources of energy than traditional fossil fuels.
- There are external costs associated with the provision of renewable energy sources: for example, noise and visual pollution from wind farms. They can also reduce property prices nearby.

Exam tip

One evaluation technique is to consider the magnitude of an event. For example, when assessing the effects of government subsidies in the renewable energy markets, this will depend upon how large the subsidies are as a proportion of total production costs for firms.

Knowledge check 43

Why might a government subsidise some goods?

Maximum price schemes

In a **maximum price** scheme, the government may impose a limit on how much prices of certain goods and services can rise. Such schemes have been used in house rental markets to protect tenants from being exploited by their landlords. Similarly, during the Second World War the government imposed maximum prices on basic food items such as milk, eggs and meat (accompanied by ration books for making purchases) to ensure a fairer distribution.

More recently, price caps were applied on various utilities such as gas and electricity. Currently there are price caps on selected rail fares and postal services. There have also been calls for the government to impose maximum wages on exceptionally high-paid public sector workers and bankers. Usually a maximum price is set below the free market price, causing shortages or an excess demand. This is shown in Figure 30 for the private house rental market. Note that a maximum price set above the free market equilibrium price will have no effect.

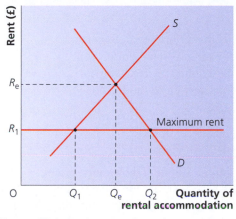

Figure 30 A maximum price scheme

> **Maximum price** A ceiling price set by the government on a good or service, above which it cannot rise. It may be enforced through government legislation.

A maximum rent of R_1 causes demand to extend from Q_e to Q_2 and supply to contract from Q_e to Q_1. It leads to an excess demand of Q_1Q_2. The shortage of private rental housing may lead to housing being allocated on a *first-come, first-served basis* or by the *sellers' preference*. Both of these forms of allocation have undesirable consequences. The government may also impose regulations on the type of customers to whom private landlords can rent: for example, vulnerable people or young mothers. However, it is more likely that this type of legislation will be used for public sector housing.

Advantages of maximum prices

- They can reduce exploitation of consumers, especially where a lack of competition exists. For example, the EU has capped the price of some mobile phone calls across member states.
- They can reduce inequality, as in the case of a salary cap on highly paid public sector workers and bankers.
- They can help people on low incomes to afford key products — for example, rental housing.

> **Knowledge check 44**
>
> Why might a government impose a maximum price in the house rental market?

Disadvantages of maximum prices

- Unintended consequences may occur: for example, government intervention distorts the operation of the price mechanism, leading to an excess demand and inefficient allocation of resources.
- In terms of the house rental market, it reduces the supply of rental property and makes the shortage worse in the long run.
- Producer surplus falls and so landlords have less income with which to invest in and maintain their property.
- Problems arise over how to allocate supply to meet the excess demand in the market, since price cannot increase. This may involve a *first-come, first-served* basis or *sellers' preference* — both of which are deemed to be unfair.
- It is difficult for the government to monitor and enforce maximum price controls in markets. There is a danger of shadow markets being created. Some people may be prepared to pay more for the good to ensure they obtain it. This is often seen with tickets at popular football matches and theatre shows.

> **Exam tip**
>
> One evaluation technique is to consider the possible difference between short-run and long-run effects of an event. For example, a maximum rent control may have few short-term effects but in the long run it is likely to lead to a serious deterioration in the quality of properties as landlords lack the funds to maintain them properly.

Minimum price schemes

In a **minimum price** scheme, the government may impose a limit on how much prices of certain goods and services can fall. Such schemes have been used in commodity markets to protect the income of farmers and also in labour markets to prevent the exploitation of workers (the national minimum wage). More recently, there have been calls for a minimum price on goods which create high external costs, such as alcohol, sugar and fizzy drinks.

Figure 31 shows the effects of a minimum price scheme in agriculture. For example, EU farmers are guaranteed a minimum price for many commodities, including sugar, wheat and barley. Usually the minimum price is set above the free market price, causing agricultural surpluses or an excess supply. These are purchased by a government agency at the **guaranteed minimum price**. Note that a minimum price set below the free market equilibrium price will have no effect.

A minimum price of P_2 causes demand to contract from Q_e to Q_1 and supply to extend from Q_e to Q_2. It leads to an excess supply of Q_1Q_2. Government expenditure on the surplus is shown by the area Q_1Q_2YW and total farm revenue increases from OP_eXQ_e to OP_2YQ_2. The excess supply is stockpiled by the government.

Knowledge check 45

What are the disadvantages of imposing a maximum price in the house rental market?

Minimum price A floor price set by the government on a good or service, below which it cannot fall. It may be enforced through government legislation.

Guaranteed minimum price Where the surplus output created is purchased by a government agency at the minimum price. The main aim of such a scheme is to protect producer incomes.

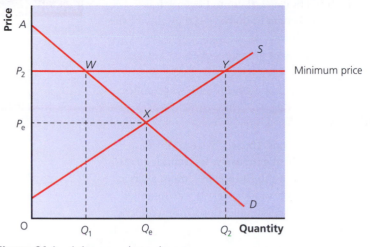

Figure 31 A minimum price scheme

Advantages of minimum prices

■ They can reduce the consumption of goods which are harmful to consumers and have high external costs, such as alcohol and sugar.

■ They encourage producers to switch to making 'healthier' drinks and foods containing less alcohol and sugar.

■ They can reduce fluctuations in food prices and so make it easier for consumers to budget their income. They also ensure food supplies even in times of poor harvest, due to the availability of surplus stockpiles.

■ A guaranteed minimum price can stabilise and increase producer incomes, leading to greater investment and employment — for example, in agriculture.

■ Food surpluses can be used as a form of international aid to developing countries.

■ A national minimum wage can reduce exploitation of labour while increasing incentives to work.

Disadvantages of minimum prices

■ Unintended consequences may occur: for example, government intervention distorts the operation of the price mechanism, leading to an excess supply and inefficient allocation of resources.

■ The price of some food and drinks will increase, which could lead to hardship for consumers on low incomes. A minimum price also reduces consumer surplus.

■ Minimum prices may be less effective in reducing consumption of alcohol and sugary drinks when demand is price inelastic.

■ A guaranteed minimum price scheme leads to the government buying up (agricultural) surpluses, which involves an opportunity cost. It may have to raise taxes or cut government spending elsewhere.

■ There are increased storage and security costs for the food surpluses. Alternatively, the food surpluses may have to be destroyed due to their perishability.

■ The food surpluses may be sold in overseas markets at very low prices. This could damage farmers in developing countries, who are unable to compete against imports of cheap food.

- Farmers are guaranteed an income, which might cause them to become less efficient over time. There is less incentive for farmers to improve the quality of the food or to keep production costs down.
- A national minimum wage may cause unemployment among workers in low-skilled labour markets.
- It is difficult for the government to monitor and enforce a minimum wage policy.

Tradable pollution permits

In 2005 the European Commission set up an Emissions Trading System (ETS) in an attempt to limit greenhouse gas emissions from heavy industry. Its main focus is to curb carbon dioxide emissions by major polluters in the European Union, such as the power generators, steel, paper, cement and ceramics industries. It was intended to include the aviation industry in the scheme in 2012, but objections from countries outside of the EU have delayed its implementation.

The ETS is a 'cap and trade' system. Each year, the European Commission allocates a set amount of carbon dioxide permits to national governments, which then divide up the allowances among the firms covered by the scheme. The system 'caps' the amount of carbon emissions for the year. The pollution permits are tradable, which means that firms can buy and sell the allowances between themselves.

Most of the **tradable pollution permits** have been given free to industry and allocated on the basis of the amount of pollution created before the scheme was introduced. However, national governments are able to retain up to 10% of carbon permits and offer them for sale, depending upon the level of scarcity. The ETS gives an incentive to firms to invest in clean technology and so reduce carbon emissions in the long term. There is also a reserve of carbon permits to enable new firms to enter those industries within the emissions trading scheme.

The ETS also allows firms to invest in schemes that reduce carbon dioxide emissions outside the European Union: for example, in India and China. The savings in carbon emissions can then be offset against their own emissions in the European Union.

Advantages of trade pollution permits

- A market is created for buying and selling carbon permits, just like other goods and services. In effect, the price mechanism is used to internalise the external costs associated with carbon emissions.
- Pollution permits can be reduced over time as part of a coordinated plan. For example, in 2008 the European Commission cut carbon allocations by 5%.
- National governments can raise funds by selling their reserve pollution permits to industry. The revenue could then be used to clean up the environment or compensate victims.
- Firms have an incentive to invest in clean technology.
- Production costs will increase for firms that exceed their pollution allowances, since they have to purchase additional permits, and this provides a source of revenue for cleaner firms that can sell their excess pollution permits.
- The ETS may act as a foundation for a global-wide scheme. It has attracted interest from developed countries outside of the EU. The north-eastern USA has set up a parallel scheme and the state of California may create its own scheme.
- Firms are able to bank their excess pollution permits for use in future years.

Knowledge check 47

What are the disadvantages of imposing a minimum price on alcohol and sugar?

Knowledge check 48

What is meant by a 'cap and trade' scheme?

Tradable pollution permits Pollution permits that can be bought and sold in a market. They are an attempt to solve the problem of pollution by creating a market for it.

Knowledge check 49

Why has the EU introduced a system of tradable pollution permits?

Disadvantages of trade pollution permits

- An information gap might cause the European Commission to issue too many carbon permits, so that there is little incentive for firms to reduce pollution. This occurred during the first phase of the ETS (2005–07) and led to a collapse in the price of carbon allowances. This reflected the absence of a means to bank spare allowances at the time.

- An information gap might cause the European Commission to issue too few carbon permits, so that production costs for EU firms increase rapidly, reducing their international competitiveness. Some firms may even relocate outside of the EU to reduce production costs.

- Disputes have arisen over the allocation of carbon permits to firms. Some companies believe they should receive larger allowances and have taken legal proceedings against the European Commission.

- Firms may pass the costs of purchasing pollution permits on to their customers, leading to higher prices of, for example, electricity, steel, glass and paper. This is more likely to happen if demand is price inelastic.

- Unintended consequences may occur: for example, there is less pressure on major polluting firms to clean up their act if it is possible to buy extra permits from elsewhere.

- EU firms may avoid investing in expensive technology to reduce their own emissions by funding cheaper carbon-offsetting schemes in developing countries.

- The price of pollution permits has fluctuated considerably since their inception in 2005. For example, the price of carbon emissions has varied from over €25 to less than €1 per ton. This has created uncertainty among firms about whether to invest heavily in carbon-reducing technology. Firms need clear guidance on what carbon prices will be for the next decade in order to determine their investment levels.

- There is a cost to the government of monitoring pollution emissions from the many companies within the scheme.

- The EU is just one part of the world. Unless all countries engage in similar carbon trading schemes, global emissions will continue to increase. In 2007, China became the world's largest carbon polluter; however, it is currently not subject to any limits.

- The valuation of pollution permits is an inexact science. Perhaps it is too important to leave to the market. Much disagreement exists over the costs of greenhouse gas emissions. Some environmental groups believe too little is being done to reduce carbon emissions. Carbon trading is simply leading to a false sense of security.

Knowledge check 50

How might the success of the EU Emissions Trading System be affected by the number of pollution permits issued?

Exam tip

One evaluation technique is to consider both advantages and disadvantages. For example, a question examining the advantages of tradable carbon permits as a means of reducing pollution invites you to consider the pros and cons of such a scheme.

State provision of public goods

It was mentioned earlier that public goods would not be provided (or would be underprovided) in a free market economy due to the free-rider problem. Once the good is provided, people are able to consume it without paying, and so private enterprise has no incentive to supply it, since making a profit would be difficult.

Consequently, the government or state tends to provide public goods in order to correct market failure. It raises funds from general taxation to pay for their provision. This is major reason why most economies are mixed economies today. Public goods involve a large element of collective consumption: for example, national defence, flood defence systems, the criminal justice system and refuse collection.

State provision of information

It was mentioned earlier that information gaps cause market failure and so require government intervention to reduce this. Today, government provision of information comes through various promotions using social media, such as the internet, television, radio, newspapers and text messages. The reasons are:

- To encourage the production and consumption of healthy goods and services: for example, fruit and vegetables, or goods that yield long-term benefits, such as pensions. Often these are underprovided in the market.
- To discourage the production and consumption of unhealthy goods and services: for example, tobacco, alcohol and drugs. Often these are overprovided in the market.
- To notify and remind people of laws for their own protection, such as wearing seatbelts in motor vehicles and not drinking alcohol and driving.

Government provision of information, along with other measures, plays an important role in reducing market failure.

Regulation

There are various forms of government **regulation** to correct market failure. In some cases direct controls are applied: for example, the Environmental Protection Act (1989) set minimum environmental standards for emissions from over 3,500 factories involved in chemical processes, waste incineration and oil refining. These firms are monitored by government pollution inspectors who have the power to impose fines and close down factories.

Regulation Government rules in markets to influence the behaviour of consumers and producers.

Advantages of regulations

- They are simple to understand: for example, legal restrictions on the age at which people can buy tobacco and alcohol.
- Limits can be imposed on the operation of firms to protect consumers: for example, a limit on the number of night air flights from Heathrow airport.
- It is possible to fine or close down companies that have abused the regulations: for example, by emitting dangerous levels of toxic waste.
- Fines act as a deterrent for both consumers and producers not to break the law. The revenue collected from fines could also be used to compensate victims.
- Regulations could require firms to restore and clean up the site after production: for example, in mining and quarrying operations.
- Regulations may help reduce the problem of asymmetric information: for example, restrictions on the sale of tobacco make it harder for young people to begin smoking, irrespective of whether they know how serious the consequences of smoking are.

Disadvantages of regulations

- Regulations can be expensive to monitor and enforce, as in the case of pollution levels imposed on firms. Administration costs can be high.
- Regulations may be set at the wrong level to correct market failure: for example, it is difficult to quantify and attach a monetary value to pollution emissions and so the social optimum position may not be reached.

- Regulations may increase the production costs of firms and make them less competitive in global markets, especially against firms in countries with few restrictions, such as China.
- Regulations may prevent the operation of the price mechanism, overruling it completely rather than working with it.
- Unintended consequences may occur. For example, in regulatory capture, the regulator acts in the interest of the firms it is meant to regulate rather than the public it is meant to protect.

Government failure

Government failure occurs when government intervention leads to an inefficient allocation of resources and a net welfare loss. There are various types of government failure, such as the distortion of price signals, unintended consequences, excessive administration costs and information gaps. This links to the previous section, which covered the disadvantages of various government measures to correct market failure.

Before being too critical of government intervention, one should note that government failure is often less serious than the market failure it tries to solve. Without government intervention, the problems associated with market failure are likely to be far greater for both consumers and producers. For example, high taxes, health campaigns and regulations on tobacco and alcohol have helped reduce demand, leading to improved public health. However, it is useful to outline some types of government failure using relevant examples.

Distortion of price signals

Maximum and minimum price controls provide good examples of the **distortion of price signals** — how government intervention distorts the operation of the price mechanism and misallocates resources.

- *Maximum price controls* lead to an excess demand or shortage, as shown in Figure 30 for rental housing. Long-term implications include a reduction in both the quality and the quantity of rental housing available, possibly leading to an increase in the number of homeless.
- *Minimum price controls* lead to an excess supply or surplus, as shown in Figure 31 for agricultural products. Long-term implications include problems of disposing of food surpluses, which are perishable and expensive to store. Minimum price schemes may also require government expenditure on the surpluses, which has an opportunity cost.

Unintended consequences

Most types of government intervention have **unintended consequences**, as revealed by the following examples:

- *Indirect taxes* may lead to the development of illegal markets: for example, tobacco and alcohol smuggling. This leads to a growth in organised crime, counterfeit products and a loss of tax revenue for the government.
- *Subsidies* may lead to firms becoming dependent on them and inefficient in production. It may also be difficult to withdraw subsidies once they are in place: for example, grants to bus and rail companies.

Government failure When government intervention leads to an inefficient allocation of resources and a net welfare loss.

Distortion of price signals The actions of government which distort the operation of the price mechanism and so misallocates resources.

Law of unintended consequences The actions of government, producers or consumers will always have effects that are unintended or unanticipated.

- *Maximum price controls* may lead to acute shortages of goods and services. The impact on private rental housing has already been discussed, but another example is a maximum wage for highly skilled workers: it could lead to a shortage of specialised workers in the banking sector that could undermine economic growth.
- *Minimum price controls* may lead to surpluses of goods and services. The impact on agricultural markets has already been discussed, but another example is a minimum wage for low-skilled workers: it could lead to unemployment as labour becomes too expensive for firms to employ.
- *Trade pollution permits* may not reduce carbon emissions so easily. For example, large polluting firms might find it easier and cheaper to buy spare permits on the market rather than invest in expensive equipment to reduce carbon emissions.
- *Regulations* may lead to regulatory capture. This is where the regulator acts in the interest of the firms, rather than of the consumers whom it is meant to protect.

Excessive administration costs

Government intervention in markets incurs **administration costs**, whether it concerns taxes, subsidies, price controls, pollution permits or regulations. Sometimes the administration costs are so high as to put into question the cost effectiveness and validity of government intervention. These costs could arise in the formulation, monitoring or enforcement of government measures. Most areas of government intervention suffer from this and several examples are offered:

- Tax administration and collection can prove difficult and expensive for government: for example, tax changes in a Budget may take a year to implement.
- Welfare benefits are difficult to calculate and monitor to make sure the right claimants receive the correct payments: for example, changes to housing benefit according to the number of spare bedrooms a claimant might have (the 'bedroom tax').
- Regulations require constant monitoring to ensure they are adhered to: for example, ensuring fishing boats do not exceed their fish catches or quotas.

Administration costs
The costs which arise in the formulation, monitoring and enforcing of government measures to correct market failure.

Information gaps

Information gaps can lead to government failure when the government lacks sufficient knowledge of the likely effects of its intervention in a particular market. This means the government could make non-rational decisions which lead to an inefficient allocation of resources and net welfare loss. We have previously shown how government intervention might fail by distorting market forces, causing unintended consequences and high administration costs. These are all linked to a lack of information in the first place concerning whether and how the government should intervene in a particular market. Several further examples are offered:

- The allocation of fish catches per boat (quotas) by EU governments appears to be set at too high a level, as the depletion of fish stocks continues. There is also the problem of fishing boats throwing back dead fish to keep within their quotas rather than risk large fines.

Government information gaps
The government has insufficient information to make rational economic decisions.

- The EU governments failed to understand how the rest of world would react to the inclusion of air travel in the Emissions Trading Scheme. The EU has been forced to postpone the extension of the ETS due to threats of retaliatory taxes from other governments.
- A government setting a very high rate of income tax for top income earners might end up reducing the total tax take due to increased tax avoidance or evasion.

Summary

- The government intervenes in different ways to correct market failure: for example, indirect taxation, subsidies, maximum and minimum prices, tradable pollution permits, provision of public goods, information and regulation.
- Indirect taxes and tradable pollution permits are used to limit production and internalise external costs to the market.
- Government subsidies are used to increase production and internalise external benefits to the market.
- Regulations are used to support the other measures and to set limits on activities that lead to market failure.
- Government failure may occur: this is where government intervention leads to an increase in inefficiency and a net welfare loss.
- Types of government failure include the distortion of price signals, unintended consequences, excessive administration costs and information gaps.
- Government failure is often less serious than the market failure it tries to solve.

Questions & Answers

Exam format

AS exam Paper 1, 'Introduction to markets and market failure', comprises 50% of the weighting for the AS examination. The paper comprises two sections: section A consists of five multiple-choice and short-answer questions; section B consists of one data-response question broken down into a number of parts including a choice from an open extended question.

The time allowed for the examination is 1 hour and 30 minutes. There are a maximum of 80 marks: 20 marks are available in section A (the multiple-choice and short-answer questions) and 60 marks in section B (the data-response question) of the exam paper. This means around 25 minutes should be spent on section A and 60 minutes on section B, leaving 5 minutes to check and amend your work.

A Level Paper 1, 'Markets and business behaviour' comprises 35% of the weighting for the A Level examination. The paper comprises three sections: section A consists of five multiple-choice and short-answer questions; section B consists of one data-response question broken down into a number of parts; section C consists of a choice of extended open-response questions.

The time allowed for the examination is 2 hours. There are a maximum of 100 marks: 25 marks are available in section A (the multiple-choice and short-answer questions), 50 marks in section B (the data-response question) and 25 marks in section C (the extended open-response question). This means around 25 minutes should be spent on section A, 60 minutes on section B and another 25 minutes on section C, leaving 10 minutes to check and amend your work.

■ Section A

Multiple-choice and short-answer questions

This part of the book contains four multiple-choice and short-answer papers. It is designed to be a key learning, revision and exam preparation resource. You should use these questions to reinforce your understanding of the specification subject matter and as practice for completing work under test conditions.

The multiple-choice and short-answer questions are similar in structure and style to the Paper 1 examination. However, in the examination each question is placed on a separate page in order to provide room for diagrams and calculations.

A maximum of 4 marks can be scored for each AS question (and 5 marks for each A Level question). Correct answers are given at the end of the section, together with mark schemes indicating how explanation marks would be awarded.

Paper 1 The nature of economics

Question 1

(a) Define the term 'production possibility frontier'.   (2 marks)

(b) The figure shows the production possibility frontier for a country moving
from *YX* to *YZ*. The most likely cause of this is: (1 mark)

   A   An increase in demand for steel.

   B   A shift of resources from food to steel production.

   C   Technological improvements in the steel industry.

   D   Exhaustion of iron ore deposits used to produce steel.

(c) What does position *W* represent for the economy?   (1 mark)

Question 2

(a) Define the term 'opportunity cost'. (1 mark)

(b) Which of the following statements concerning opportunity cost is correct? (1 mark)

- **A**   It is always measured in money terms.
- **B**   It occurs in market economies but not mixed economies.
- **C**   It indicates that resources are infinite.
- **D**   It occurs for both consumers and producers.

(c) Referring to an example, explain what is meant by the basic economic problem. (2 marks)

Question 3

(a) Define the term 'division of labour'. (1 mark)

(b) A fast-food restaurant carries out labour specialisation in the production of burgers. The purpose of this is to: (1 mark)

- **A**   Achieve benefits from the division of labour.
- **B**   Increase the total costs of production.
- **C**   Achieve benefits from economies of scale.
- **D**   Increase employment for those who want a job.

(c) Outline two possible disadvantages from the division of labour. (2 marks)

Question 4

(a) A free market economy differs from a mixed economy in the following way: (1 mark)

- **A**   Business is organised to produce necessities rather than luxuries.
- **B**   All resources are allocated by the price mechanism.
- **C**   Essential services such as healthcare and education are provided free to all and funded from taxation.
- **D**   Most resources are owned and controlled by the government.

(b) Briefly explain three advantages of a free market economy. (3 marks)

Question 5

Statement 1: Tax now forms 86% of the price of a packet of cigarettes.

Statement 2: The tax on cigarettes should be increased further.

(a) Which one of the following best describes the two statements above? (1 mark)

	Statement 1	Statement 2
A	Positive	Positive
B	Normative	Positive
C	Positive	Normative
D	Normative	Normative

(b) With reference to the tax on tobacco, explain the role of value judgements in economic decision making. (3 marks)

Paper 2 How markets work

Question 1

The following table shows the demand and supply schedules for a good.
(You may use the blank column in your explanation.)

Price per unit (£)	Quantity demanded (units)	Quantity supplied (units)	New quantity demanded (units)
10	200	1,800	
9	400	1,600	
8	600	1,400	
7	800	1,200	
6	1,000	1,000	
5	1,200	800	
4	1,400	600	

(a) What is the original equilibrium price and quantity? (1 mark)

(b) An increase in demand of 400 units at every price level will cause: (1 mark)

    A An increase in the equilibrium price but not quantity.

    B An increase in the equilibrium quantity but not price.

    C An increase in the equilibrium price and quantity.

    D Equilibrium price and quantity to remain constant.

(c) Calculate price elasticity of supply following an increase in price from £6 to £8. Show your workings. (2 marks)

Question 2

(a) What is the formula for price elasticity of demand? (1 mark)

(b) The owner of a cinema decides to reduce the price of each ticket from £10 to £5. This causes ticket sales to increase for each showing from 200 to 400.

The best estimate for price elasticity of demand is: (1 mark)

    A −0.5

    B −1.0

    C −1.5

    D −2.0

(c) Explain two factors which might affect the price elasticity of demand for visiting the cinema. (2 marks)

Question 3

(a) Define the term 'subsidy'.   (1 mark)

(b) The diagram shows a unit subsidy placed on rail travel between London and
Bath, shifting the supply curve from S_1 to S_2. Which of the following is correct?   (1 mark)

    A   Consumer surplus increases by P_1P_2FX.

    B   The total subsidy area is OP_2FQ_2.

    C   Producer surplus increases to P_1XY.

    D   The rail fare falls by the same amount as the unit subsidy.

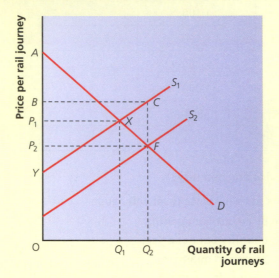

(c) Outline two likely reasons why the government provides subsidies for rail travel.   (2 marks)

Question 4

The table shows the income elasticities of demand for selected UK holiday destinations.

Holiday destination	Income elasticity of demand
Bournemouth	2.0
Newquay	0.6
Margate	−0.4

(a) It may be deduced from the data in the table that: (1 mark)

    A   All the holiday destinations are normal goods.

    B   Holidays in Bournemouth are price elastic in demand.

    C   A decrease in real income will cause a decrease in demand for holidays
in Newquay.

    D   There is a negative cross elasticity of demand for holidays in Margate.

(b) Using examples, distinguish between normal and inferior goods.   (3 marks)

Question 5

The table shows the demand and supply schedules for a luxury range of caviar.
(You may use the blank column for your explanation.)

Price per unit (£)	Quantity demanded (boxes)	Quantity supplied (boxes)	New quantity supplied (boxes)
50	120	240	
40	140	220	
30	160	200	
20	180	180	
10	200	160	

(a) Define the term 'indirect tax'. (1 mark)

(b) If the government introduces an indirect tax of £20 per box of caviar, what is the new equilibrium price? (1 mark)

(c) The tax revenue obtained will be: (show your workings) (2 marks)
   - **A** £4,400
   - **B** £3,600
   - **C** £3,200
   - **D** £2,800

Paper 3 Market failure

Question 1

(a) All of the following are examples of market failure except: (1 mark)
   - **A** External costs and benefits
   - **B** Underprovision of public goods
   - **C** Information gaps between consumers and producers
   - **D** Unemployment created by the national minimum wage

(b) Explain why a coastal flood defence scheme is unlikely to be provided in a free market economy. (3 marks)

Question 2

(a) A negative externality exists when: (1 mark)
   - **A** The consumption of a product provides benefits to third parties
   - **B** The social cost exceeds the private cost in production
   - **C** Costs are internalised by the price mechanism
   - **D** The social cost is less than the private cost in consumption

(b) The diagram shows the market for fracked gas. Assuming no government intervention, explain why a welfare loss will be created in the market.   (2 marks)

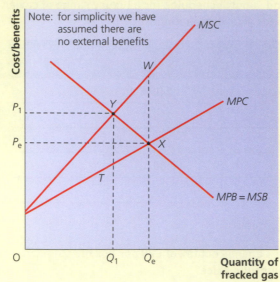

(c) Outline an external cost that might arise from fracking gas.   (1 mark)

Question 3

(a) External benefits arise from the university education market since: (1 mark)

    A   The price mechanism directly takes account of these benefits

    B   Tuition fees are greater than the benefits

    C   Social benefits exceed private benefits

    D   Tuition fees equal the private benefits

(b) The diagram shows the market for university education. Assume there are no external costs and no government intervention. The equilibrium quantity is Q_e. Explain how it is possible to increase welfare.   (2 marks)

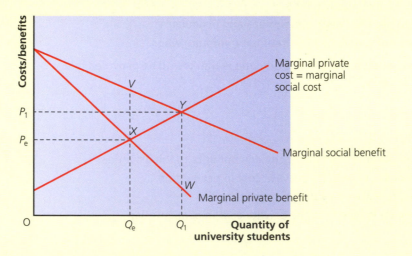

(c) Outline an external benefit that might arise from university education.   (1 mark)

Question 4

(a) Over one-third of British holiday makers fail to take out travel insurance when taking foreign holidays. A likely reason for the underconsumption of holiday travel insurance is: (1 mark)

   A   The provision of government subsidies to holiday travel firms

   B   Holiday makers have perfect information about travel insurance

   C   The price of holiday travel insurance has fallen over recent years

   D   An information gap exists in the holiday travel insurance market

(b) The graph shows UK obesity rates between 1993 and 2012. With reference to imperfect market information, explain the possible causes of the trend shown. (3 marks)

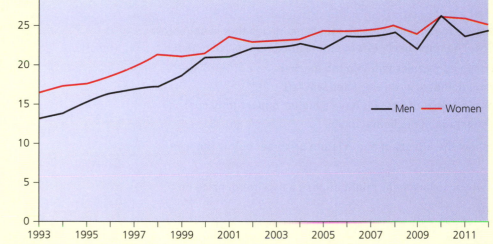

UK obesity rates for adult population, 1993–2012

Source: *Health Survey for England, 2012* (Health and Social Care Information Centre)

Question 5

(a) Market failure will occur if: (1 mark)

   A   Government intervention in healthcare leads to a misallocation of resources

   B   Workers do not make adequate pension contributions to fund their retirement

   C   Firms exit a market in response to a decrease in demand for their goods

   D   External benefits from the provision of education are internalised by the price mechanism

(b) Define the term 'market failure'. (1 mark)

(c) Wind power from wind turbines provides enough energy for more than 5 million homes in the UK. Explain one external benefit and one external cost from generating energy by wind power. (2 marks)

Paper 4 Government intervention

Question 1

(a) Tradable pollution permits are more likely to be effective in reducing carbon dioxide emissions within the European Union if: (1 mark)

    A   Firms find it difficult to introduce clean technology in production

    B   Demand exceeds supply of pollution permits

    C   It is difficult to monitor carbon emissions from firms

    D   The market price of pollution permits is very low

(b) Outline what is meant by a 'cap and trade' system of pollution permits. (1 mark)

(c) Explain two reasons why EU tradable pollution permits may be ineffective in reducing global carbon emissions. (2 marks)

Question 2

(a) A government imposes a maximum price on medicinal drugs that is set below the free market price. The most likely effect of this maximum price is that: (1 mark)

    A   New medicinal drug companies will join the market

    B   The quantity of medicinal drugs demanded will fall

    C   The purchase of medicinal drugs will have a higher opportunity cost

    D   There will be a shortage of medicinal drugs

(b) Draw a diagram to show the effects of a maximum price set below the free market price. (2 marks)

(c) Outline one reason why a government might impose a maximum price on medicinal drugs. (1 mark)

Question 3

(a) The government is considering introducing a minimum price for alcohol of 50p per unit. Assuming this price is above the free market price, the most likely effect is to cause: (1 mark)

    A   A decrease in consumption

    B   A decrease in market price

    C   Equilibrium in the market

    D   A shortage of alcohol

(b) Draw a diagram to show the effects of a minimum price set above the free market price. (2 marks)

(c) Outline one reason why a government might impose a minimum price on alcohol. (1 mark)

Question 4

(a) The diagram shows the impact of a specific tax on air travel. Which of the following is correct? (1 mark)

   A   The tax paid by consumers is area P_1P_2WX
   B   The total tax collected is area VP_2WT
   C   The tax paid by producers is area P_1XTV
   D   The total tax collected is area OP_2WQ_2

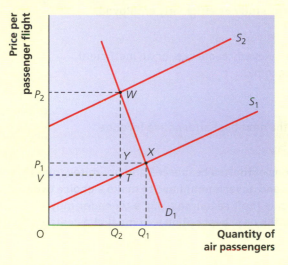

(b) With reference to the diagram, explain why most of the specific tax is paid by consumers. (3 marks)

Question 5

(a) 86% of the price of tobacco comprises tax. The most likely reason for the government imposing such a high level of tax is to: (1 mark)

   A   Maintain employment in the tobacco industry
   B   Internalise the external benefits of tobacco consumption
   C   Maintain a maximum price for tobacco
   D   Internalise the external costs of tobacco consumption

(b) Various regulations are imposed on the sale and consumption of tobacco. These include a ban on smoking in enclosed public buildings, restrictions on the age limit for purchasing tobacco and the introduction of plain packaging.

Explain the disadvantages of regulations as a means of reducing tobacco consumption. (3 marks)

Answers to multiple-choice and short-answer questions

Paper 1 The nature of economics

Question 1

(a) Production possibility frontier is the maximum potential output for an economy/when all its resources are fully or efficiently employed. (1+1 marks)

(b) Correct answer C. (1 mark)

(c) Position *W* means there are unemployed resources, or an inefficient allocation of resources in the economy. 1 mark

Question 2

(a) Opportunity cost is the value of the next best alternative forgone. (1 mark)

(b) Correct answer D. (1 mark)

(c) The basic economic problem is one of limited resources and unlimited human wants/so consumers, producers and government have to make a choice over how to spend their funds or allocate their resources, e.g. a teenager may have £20 to spend on a T-shirt or the next best option — a meal at a restaurant. (1+1 marks)

Question 3

(a) Division of labour is when production is broken down into different operations and labour allocated to each one. (1 mark)

(b) Correct answer A. (1 mark)

(c) Disadvantages of division of labour include: boredom from repetitive work that might reduce productivity/higher staff turnover from the job/interdependence creates vulnerability in production. (1+1 marks)

Question 4

(a) Correct answer B. (1 mark)

(b) Advantages of a free market economy include: competition leads to increased efficiency in production and lower prices for consumers/greater incentive for firms to improve product quality/increase in consumer choice/profit motive encourages firms to invest and take risks/labour has incentive to work harder and gain higher earnings. (1+1+1 marks)

Question 5

(a) Correct answer C. (1 mark)

(b) Value judgements are normative statements which cannot be tested as true or false/many people believe the tax on cigarettes should increase further since it creates many costs to society such as a decrease in life expectancy/increase in illness and inability to work/pressures on the National Health Service/passive smoking/smokers may not be acting rationally. (1+1+1 marks).

Paper 2: How markets work

Question 1

(a) Equilibrium price refers to the price level in a market where the quantity demand equals the quantity supply. In this case the equilibrium price is £6 and the equilibrium quantity 1,000 units. (1 mark)

(b) Correct answer C. Price rises to £7 and quantity to 1,200 units. (1 mark)

(c) Price elasticity of supply is 1.2 (1 mark); workings are 40% ÷ 33% (1 mark)

Question 2

(a) Formula: $PED = \% \Delta QD \div \% \Delta P$ (1 mark)

(b) Correct answer D. (1 mark)

(c) PED for cinema tickets is affected by substitutes (such as downloading online films, which could increase elasticity of demand); also the percentage of income spent on cinema tickets (quite low for most consumers and so could be inelastic in demand). (1+1 marks)

Question 3

(a) A subsidy is a grant provided to firms to increase production and lower the price of a particular good or service. (1 mark)

(b) Correct answer A. (1 mark)

(c) Government may provide rail subsidies to: reduce road congestion and associated external costs/provide funds for rail firms to increase investment/make rail travel more accessible for low-income groups. (1+1 marks)

Question 4

(a) Correct answer C. (1 mark)

(b) Normal goods have a positive YED whereas inferior goods have a negative YED (1 mark); a normal good is where a rise in income causes a rise in demand and an inferior good is where a rise in income causes a fall in demand (1 mark); holidays to Bournemouth and Newquay are normal goods but holidays to Margate are inferior goods (1 mark). (3 marks).

Question 5

(a) Indirect tax: a tax placed on the expenditure of a good or service. (1 mark)

(b) The new equilibrium price is £30 and the equilibrium quantity is 160 boxes. (1 mark)

(c) Correct answer C (1 mark); quantity of 160 × tax per box of £20 = £3,200. (3 marks)

Paper 3: Market failure

Question 1

(a) Correct answer D. (1 mark)

(b) A coastal flood defence scheme is unlikely to be provided in a free market economy, since it is a public good characterised by non-rivalry and non-excludability in consumption; this leads to a free-rider problem where people can consume a good for free once it has been provided/so no incentive for firms to provide it as they cannot make a profit. (1+1+1 marks)

Question 2

(a) Correct answer B. (1 mark)

(b) A welfare loss of *WXY* will be created, since the free market output of OQ_e exceeds the social optimum output of OQ_1; for output slice Q_eQ_1, social costs of Q_1Q_eWY exceed social benefits of Q_1Q_eXY, or, it is possible to increase society's welfare by reducing output to OQ_1 where $MSB = MSC$. (1+1 marks)

(c) Air or noise pollution/visual eyesore which reduce local property prices/possible damage to water supply. (1 mark)

Question 3

(a) Correct answer C. (1 mark)

(b) It is possible to increase welfare by *VYX*/the quantity of university students is increased from OQ_e to OQ_1; for output slice Q_eQ_1, social benefits of Q_eQ_1YV exceed social costs of Q_eQ_1YX. (1+1 marks)

(c) Increased labour productivity of graduates means that firms can gain more profits from employing them/increased tax revenues for government as graduates typically earn more than non-graduates. (1 mark)

Question 4

(a) Correct answer D. (1 mark)

(b) Data reference on the trend of an increase in obesity among men and women/one cause is the lack of consumer knowledge on the calorie and fat content of various foods and drink/this may lead to overconsumption of high-fat foods such as cakes and sweets compared to daily requirements/a lack of knowledge on the importance of exercise to burn the calories. (any 3 points 1+1+1 marks)

Question 5

(a) Correct answer B. (1 mark)

(b) Market failure is when the price mechanism causes an inefficient allocation of resources and so leads to a net welfare loss. (1 mark)

(c) External benefits from wind power include: reduction in pollution from use of fossil fuels/increases the provision of fossil fuel energy for future generations; external costs include: visual eyesore/reduction in local property prices/noise pollution/damage to birds. (1+1 marks)

Paper 4: Government intervention

Question 1

(a) Correct answer B. (1 mark)

(b) A 'cap' means there is a limit to the number of pollution permits issued by the EU each year; the term 'trade' means these permits can be bought and sold in the market. (1 mark)

(c) Reasons include: EU trade pollution permits only cover EU industry whereas biggest carbon polluters are in other parts of the world such as China and the USA/too may permits may be issued, which lower their price, so there is little incentive for firms to invest in clean technology. (1+1 marks)

Question 2

(a) Correct answer D. (1 mark)

(b) Diagram depicting the maximum price line set below the free market equilibrium price/with the quantity of excess demand identified (as shown by Figure 30, page 49). (1+1 marks)

(c) The main reason for a maximum price is to prevent exploitation of consumers by drugs companies, which might otherwise charge very high prices. (1 mark)

Question 3

(a) Correct answer A. (1 mark)

(b) Diagram depicting the minimum price line set above the free market equilibrium price/with the quantity of excess supply identified (as shown by Figure 31, page 51). (1+1 marks)

(c) The main reason for a minimum price on alcohol is to reduce consumption of good which yields high levels of private and external costs such as damage to health through alcoholism and greater incidence of crime. (1 mark)

Question 4

(a) Correct answer B. (1 mark)

(b) The consumer pays tax area P_1P_2WY and the producer pays tax area P_1YTV; demand appears relatively price inelastic and so most of the tax is passed on to consumers via higher air fares. (1+1+1 marks)

Question 5

(a) Correct answer D. (1 mark)

(b) Disadvantages of tobacco regulations include: difficulty of monitoring and enforcing them, e.g. smoking in pubs and restaurants; adults may purchase cigarettes for children; unintended consequences may arise, e.g. some children believing it is 'cool to smoke' since it is illegal; plain packaging may make it easier to produce counterfeit cigarettes. (1+1+1 marks)

Section B

Data-response and open-extended questions

Structure of the questions

AS: The data-response question on this paper comprises six sub-questions which total 60 marks. The first five, labelled (a) to (e), are compulsory and add to 40 marks. The last sub-question offers a choice from two, (f) or (g). This is the open-extended question on the paper, offering up to 20 marks. Question 1 on the housing market follows this structure.

A Level: The data-response question on this paper comprises five compulsory sub-questions labelled (a) to (e), which total 50 marks. Question 2 on proposals for fracking in the UK follows this structure. The final part of this paper, section C, is one from a choice of two open-extended questions offering up to 25 marks. Question 3 on minimum pricing and taxation of sugar is an example here.

There is a 'levels'-based approach to marking the data-response and open-extended questions, particularly those with a high mark tariff. This enables a variety of different approaches in student answers to be valid rather than solely requiring specific points that are stated on the mark scheme. It means the examiner makes an initial assessment of the quality of an answer and places it at a level ranging from 1 to 4. The examiner's judgement is then refined to award a more precise mark within that level. It is recommended that you refer to the Levels descriptors provided in the sample assessment materials for Economics produced by Edexcel at www.edexcel.com/quals/gce/gce15/economics/Pages/default.aspx

In addition, a levels-based mark scheme is often broken down into two further parts: the first focuses on 'knowledge, application and analysis' marks and the second relates to 'evaluation'. Evaluation questions are typically broken down like this. The command words used for evaluation questions are: *examine, evaluate, assess, discuss, comment upon* and *to what extent*. Any of these words in the question indicate that you should demonstrate some critical understanding of the issues being discussed.

Each sub-question here is followed by a comment, which is preceded by the icon ⓔ. This gives general guidance on how the question should be approached. You are advised to attempt the questions yourself before you read the sample student answer supplied. Student answers are followed by detailed comments which show you exactly what is rewarded and how the answer might have been improved. These comments are preceded by the icon ⓔ.

Question 1 The housing market

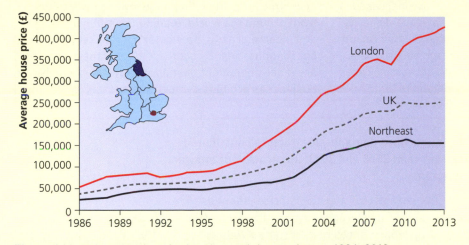

Figure 1 Mean house prices for London and the northeast, 1986–2013

Source: www.ons.gov.uk/ons/rel/hpi/house-price-index/january-2014/sty-regional-house-prices.html

Figure 2 Comparison of average house prices, annual earnings, employment growth and population density for London and northeast England, 2014

Region	Average property price (£)	Average earnings per employee (£)	Number employed	Employment change, 2007–14 (%)	Population density (per square mile)
Northeast	150,000	24,440	1,111,000	–6.5	780
London	492,000	34,216	5,516,000	15.8	13,510

Source: www.ons.gov.uk/ons/rel/hpi/house-price-index/january-2014/sty-regional-house-prices.html

Extract 1 Rising house prices

Average house prices in the UK increased from £100,000 in the year 2000 to £250,000 by 2013. They are set to increase further in 2014, leading to fears of a 'property bubble'. Both demand-side and supply-side factors are to blame. Until the recession in 2008–10, real incomes rose strongly, supported by an increase in immigration from eastern Europe. Record low mortgage interest rates have played an important part in stimulating recovery in the housing market. There are also severe constraints from house building regulations and a shortage of skilled building workers. Delivery times for bricks and other building materials have also increased, forcing firms to look to imports. However, the government has responded by increasing training programmes in the building industry.

Rising house prices should be bad news for first-time buyers. However, the government launched a 'Help to buy' scheme, enabling first-time buyers to obtain mortgages of up to 95% of the value of the property. This means only a 5% cash deposit is required compared to the usual 40%. Banks are more willing to provide mortgages under the scheme, since the government guarantees the house loan. Some £12 billion of house loans are guaranteed by the government.

Questions & Answers

(a) With reference to Extract 1, explain how 'demand-side' factors contributed to the rise in UK house prices between 2000 and 2013. Illustrate your answer with a demand and supply diagram.

(5 marks)

ⓔ You should focus on 'demand-side' causes of rising house prices mentioned in the extract. There is no need to explain the 'supply-side' causes, as no evaluation marks are available. Ensure that a diagram is offered or your marks will be capped. Also make explicit use of the house price data.

(b) With reference to Extract 1, discuss whether the supply of new-build housing is likely to be price elastic or price inelastic.

(10 marks)

ⓔ Try to consider the key concept underlying the question: namely, price elasticity of supply. There is evidence in the extract about skilled labour and building material shortages, which suggest that supply is price inelastic. There are 4 marks available for evaluation.

(c) With reference to Extract 1, explain the likely impact of the government 'Help to buy' scheme on first-time buyers.

(4 marks)

ⓔ Use the information in Extract 1 and try and add value. Keep things simple. You are not expected to be an expert on government schemes to support house ownership.

(d) With reference to Figure 2, calculate:

　(i) The ratio of average house prices between London and the northeast.
　(ii) The ratio of average earnings between London and the northeast.

　　　Outline your findings.

(6 marks)

ⓔ There will often be a quantitative question in the data-response section of the paper. Make sure you can calculate ratios and explain the results.

(e) With reference to the information provided, examine three possible reasons why average house prices differ between London and the northeast.

(15 marks)

ⓔ Include data from Figures 1 and 2 in your answer. Ideas from Extract 2 should also be used, although you may add your own too. Be prepared to offer two or three evaluation points for 15-mark questions. There are 6 marks available for evaluation.

EITHER:

(f) To what extent might the introduction of maximum rent controls on private rental housing alleviate the housing shortage? (20 marks)

e The command phrase 'To what extent' invites you to consider the degree to which you agree with the statement, supporting your argument with evidence. Be prepared to challenge the statement — you might not agree with it. It is useful to look at both sides of the argument. There are 14 knowledge, application and analysis marks and 6 evaluation marks available.

OR:

(g) Discuss measures the government and monetary authorities could take to limit the growth in house prices. (20 marks)

e The command word 'discuss' invites you to consider the effectiveness of various measures to limit house price growth. The question mentions 'monetary authorities', so it is possible to refer to the role of the Bank of England in raising interest rates. Government measures could include abolishing the 'Help to buy' scheme, higher stamp duties on buying property and subsidies to build more social housing. There are 14 knowledge, application and analysis marks and 6 evaluation marks available.

Student answer

(a) UK average house prices have increased by £150,000 between 2000 and 2013, a huge 150% increase. **a** On the demand side, rising incomes, immigration from eastern Europe and record low interest rates are the causes. Rising real incomes and record low interest rates mean the monthly repayments on house loans are more affordable and so this encourages home ownership. The rise in immigration has put added pressure on a limited housing stock and so driven up its price. **b** The diagram shows the demand for housing increasing from D_1 to D_2 and price increasing from P_1 to P_2. **c**

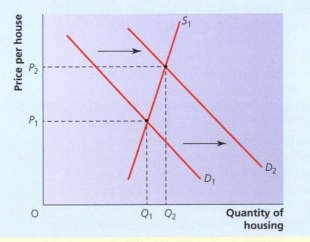

ℯ 5/5 marks awarded. a The student explicitly refers to the data concerning the rise in house prices (1 mark). **b** Three demand-side reasons are given for the rise in house prices with some development (1+1 marks). **c** A relevant diagram is shown, depicting an increase in demand and higher equilibrium price (1+1 marks).

(b) Price elasticity of supply refers to the responsiveness of supply to the change in the price of a good. Information in the extract indicates that supply of new housing is likely to be price inelastic (where the proportional rise in supply is less than the proportional rise in price). **a**

There appear to be three constraints on supply: first the tight planning regulations on building new housing, especially in urban areas. It takes a long time for developers to gain approval for building new homes and often there are objections by local residents who want to maintain access to open spaces; second, the extract refers to a shortage of skilled building workers such as bricklayers and plumbers — it means developers have to offer high wages and wait for more people to be trained before responding to increased house prices; third, there is a shortage of building materials which further delays the ability of developers to respond to rising house prices. It increases the average time taken to build housing. **b**

To evaluate, it is not surprising that supply is inelastic given a 150% increase in house prices between 2000 and 2013. It would be extremely difficult for new-builds to keep up with such a fast rate, particularly given the nature of construction which requires many different types of skilled labour to be co-ordinated to do specific jobs at certain times in the building process. **c** However, in the long run supply may become less price inelastic (more elastic) since the housing shortage has become so acute that government may relax planning regulations to speed up new developments. Furthermore, the government has increased the number of training courses for builders to overcome skilled labour shortages. Once qualified, this will make it easier for firms to build new houses. Finally, the shortage of building materials can be offset by importing them, especially as the UK is part of the single European market and so no import taxes are levied from this region. **d**

ℯ 10/10 marks awarded. a The student defines price elasticity of supply and explains the meaning of price inelastic supply. It is useful to make the meaning of both terms clear to the examiner as 2 marks are available. Quite often the latter is missed out in student answers (1+1 marks). **b** Three reasons are offered to explain why new housing is likely to be price inelastic in supply. All three factors come from Extract 1 and are developed further. It is important to add value to answers rather than just repeating the information from the extract (2+2+2 marks). Note that a maximum of 6 knowledge, application and analysis marks are available from the 8 marks identified. **c** and **d** Two evaluation points are offered, one discussing the magnitude of the house price increase and the other considering the significance of the time period. Both of these are valid evaluation techniques (2+2 marks).

(c) The help to buy scheme will make it easier for first-time buyers to get on the property ladder. They only need to provide 5% cash deposit and so this should be easier and quicker to save up for. Previously, the banks were demanding up to 40% cash deposit, which took far long for people to save for, especially if house prices continue to increase. **a** Furthermore, any first-time buyers are at an early stage of their career and so presumably they have not reached their maximum earnings potential. This could make it really hard to save up and buy a property, especially when interest rates are likely to rise in future, increasing the monthly mortgage repayments. **b**

e **4/4 marks awarded.** **a** Easier and quicker for first-time buyers to save up the deposit (1 mark), especially when property prices are rising (1 mark). **b** First-time buyers at an early stage in their career and have not maximised earnings potential — so a real help to buy property (2 marks).

(d) (i) Ratio of average house prices between London and the North-East is 3.28 (£492,000 ÷ £150,000). **a** This means the average house in London is more than three times that for the northeast of England. One could buy three houses in the northeast and still have money left over compared to buying a house in London.

(ii) Ratio of average earnings between London and the northeast is 1.4 (£34,216 ÷ £24,440). **b** This suggests that average earnings can only partly explain the disparity in regional house prices and that there are other important factors to consider such as net regional migration and availability of building land. **c**

e **6/6 marks awarded.** **a** Calculation of ratio of house prices 3.28 (2 marks). **b** Calculation of ratio of average earnings 1.4 (2 marks). **c** Comment that earnings differences can only partly account for the house price disparities and that other factors should be considered, such as net regional migration and availability of building land (2 marks).

(e) Figure 1 shows an increase in the gap between average regional house prices for London and the northeast since the mid-1990s. **a** The most notable increase in this gap has been since 2010 where the London property market has clearly soared — unlike that for northeast England (which recorded a small decline in house prices compared to the pre-financial crisis). Recovery from the recession has yet to reach northeast England and it may take more time for consumer and business confidence to return here.

The first reason for house price disparities could be due to the differences in regional income and wealth. Figure 2 shows that on average, people earn a higher income in London (£34,216) than the northeast (£24,440) and so can afford to take out bigger mortgages and pay more for houses. Also there is a lot of wealth built up in houses over many years in London. When people move homes in London they probably have a lot of wealth in the house to take with them to put as a deposit on their new home. **b**

A second reason might be due to the greater scarcity of land for building on in London compared to the northeast. There are very tight planning restrictions in London since it is already a heavily urbanised area and so not much land becomes available to build on. Figure 2 shows that London's population density is very high at 13,510 per square mile compared to just 780 per square mile in the northeast. It means demand tends to exceed supply, pushing up the price of land. In the northeast there is more land available to build on so the price of this is lower, reducing the costs of building houses. This will lead to lower house prices. The higher level of demand compared to supply between the two regions is shown in the diagram. The house price equilibrium is much higher in London. The diagrams below show the difference in regional house prices between London and the northeast. c

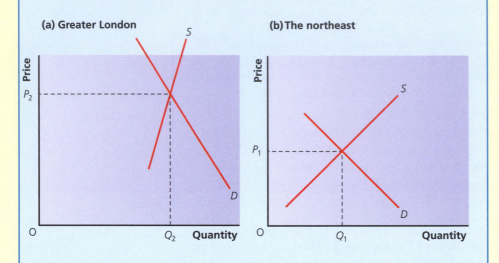

(a) Greater London

(b) The northeast

A third reason could be due to the nature of the regional economies: London is heavily dependent on financial services, business consultancy and tourism. These are growth industries which attract a lot of inward investment and so increase the demand for property in general. Figure 2 indicates that employment grew by 15.8% between 2007 and 2014 in London. On the other hand, the northeast depends more on traditional manufacturing industries that are growing slowly. Consequently there is less employment, investment and demand for property. Figure 2 reveals that employment actually fell by 6.5% between 2007 and 2014. Consequently there is less pressure on property prices to rise. d

In evaluation, one could note that differences in average earnings do not appear that significant. However, in reality, there are enormous levels of inequality in London with many very wealthy people, including those who come from abroad. The effect has been to drive up property prices at the top end of the market and over time this has gradually filtered down to ordinary sized properties across London. e

Another evaluation point is that enormous differences in house prices exist within each region, depending upon the areas considered. For example, average house prices in the London boroughs of Kensington and Chelsea exceed £1 million whereas those in Dagenham and Barking are closer to £250,000. It may be a bit early to talk about a north–south divide in the UK. **f**

A final evaluation point is that other factors help explain regional house price differences, such as unemployment rates, net migration flows, the cost of living and distance from major markets. Further information on these would help to determine their significance. **g**

e **15/15 marks awarded.** **a** Reference to the widening regional house price gap in Figure 1 (1 mark). **b, c, d** Three causes of regional house price differences explained with reference to the data (3+3+3 marks); note that a maximum of 9 knowledge, application and analysis marks are available from the 10 marks identified. **e, f, g** Three evaluative comments are offered (2+2+2 marks). It is acceptable to offer evaluation points at the end of the answer, or as one proceeds with each knowledge, application and analysis point. It is always helpful to let the examiner know when you are offering an evaluation point.

(f) Rent controls are a form of maximum pricing. This is where a maximum rent or price ceiling is set for rental property each month usually backed by government legislation. Such a measure appears to have unintended consequences and it is unlikely to alleviate the housing shortage since there is less incentive for private landlords to rent out their properties at lower prices. It also means that demand for rental properties will rise due to the lower charge, leading to excess demand. This is shown by the diagram where the government sets a maximum rent of OR_1 which is below the free market rent of OR_e. Supply contracts to OQ_1 and demand extends to OQ_2 leading to a shortage of private rental property of Q_1Q_2. It seems that government intervention distorts the operation of the price mechanism and leads to an inefficient allocation of resources, especially in the long run if the rent controls remain. **a**

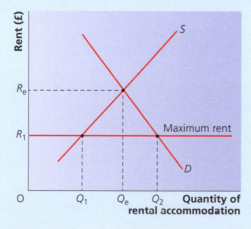

Rent controls could also damage the quality of the housing stock as landlords have less income to invest and maintain their property. It could lead to the provision of very poor quality housing and create slum areas. Job losses might also be felt in the building maintenance sector. **b**

Rent controls also raise problems over how to allocate the supply of housing to meet excess demand in the market. Different options exist such as allocating rental property according to a first-come, first-served basis or by sellers' preference. The former could lead to a stampede of potential tenants and the latter is open to abuse from the landlord. **c**

Finally there are problems of government monitoring and enforcing maximum rent controls. There are millions of rental properties and it will take a large number of inspectors a long time at great cost to check these on a regular basis. There is a real danger of a shadow market or hidden market being created where some potential renters (tenants) pay more than the maximum rent to ensure they obtain a desirable property to live. Such illegal markets place tenants at risk from exploitation. **d**

However, in evaluation of rent controls, they do have a role to play in alleviating the housing shortage. They can reduce exploitation of tenants and ensure that rents are set at affordable levels. It also means that people on relatively low incomes might be able to afford to rent property so that it helps to reduce inequality. **e** There is every reason to believe that the supply of rental accommodation is price inelastic so there might only be a small reduction in rental properties on the market. Landlords might have little alternative other than to sell their property. On the other hand, the demand for rental property could be price elastic and so more people come forward looking to rent. This means the housing shortage will remain. **f** Another point to consider is the rent control in relation to the free market price. If a maximum rent is set above the free market rent, then there is no effect in the market. One might expect that a nationally imposed maximum rent will exceed the average rental prices in the northeast but be well below them in the London region. It raises the issue of whether to set regional rent controls — but this just adds to the complexity of it. **g** It might be better for the government to look elsewhere to solve the housing shortage — for example, by relaxing planning regulations or undertaking a major public house building programme. Mortgage subsidies and tax relief could be other options, but these have their own problems. **h**

e **20/20 marks awarded.** **a** The student starts by defining the key concept in the question: namely, 'maximum rent controls' — this is always a good idea (1 mark). This is supported by diagrammatic analysis and explanation of how rent controls could worsen the housing shortage (3 marks for diagram and 2 marks for explanation). **b, c, d** There is consideration of other problems associated with maximum pricing, applied to the house rental market (4+4+4 marks). Note that a maximum of 14 knowledge, application and analysis marks are available from the 18 marks identified.

e, f These are evaluative comments; they consider positive aspects of rent controls and make use of concepts such as price elasticity of supply and demand (3+3 marks); **g** the student discusses the maximum price set in relation to the free market price (3 marks) and **h** raises the prospect of alternative measures to alleviate the housing shortage (2 marks). Note that a maximum of 6 evaluation marks are available from the 11 marks identified. Clearly this is a superior answer.

e Total score: 60/60 marks = a top grade A

(g) There are various measures the government could take to reduce the growth in house prices over the next few years. The most obvious measure is to abolish the 'Help to buy' scheme mentioned in Extract 1. This will force people to take more time to increase their savings for a larger cash deposit before buying a house. Banks are also less likely to lend money for house purchases due to the increased risk of default by borrowers. Scrapping 'Help to buy' will reduce the number of new people entering the home owner property market and so limit demand pressures at the bottom end. **a**

A second measure is for the government to subsidise house building firms in some manner so that more are built and offered for sale at lower prices. The government will need to obtain a guarantee beforehand of the price which this housing would be sold for so that consumers gain some benefit. A subsidy diagram is shown for the private housing market. The effect is to increase supply to S_2 and reduce price to P_2. It should enable more people to get on to the home ownership ladder. The total subsidy is area $GLRP_2$. The portion of subsidy going to consumers is P_eTRP_2 and to producers P_eTLG. **b**

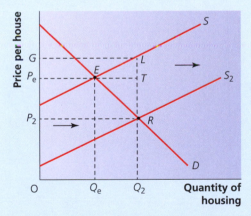

A third measure is to rely upon the monetary authorities at the Bank of England. There are concerns that house prices might spiral out of control leading to a price bubble that will burst. To prevent this from happening the Bank could increase the Base rate of interest which has been at a record low of 0.5% for almost six years since 2009. This will have a knock-on effect for interest rates throughout the financial markets. Higher rates of interest on house loans will make it more expensive for people to buy property and also for existing borrowers to maintain their repayments. Consequently, this double effect will help reduce demand in the housing market and so limit the growth in prices. **c**

ⓔ 14/20 marks awarded. ⓐ The student considers three measures, which is appropriate for a 20-mark question. The first makes good use of Extract 1 concerning the 'Help to buy' scheme', which the student suggests could be scrapped (4 marks). **ⓑ** The second measure focuses on subsidies to house builders and is supported by diagrammatic analysis (3 marks for diagram and 3 marks for explanation). **ⓒ** The third measure considers an increase in interest rates from the Bank of England and how this might affect existing and new house borrowers (4 marks).

The main problem with this answer is the failure to offer any evaluative comments. The student should offer at least two points in order to gain the 6 evaluation marks available. For example, the 'Help to buy' scheme is fairly limited in terms of the number of people able to get house loans. It does not have much effect on overall house prices. Then there is the problem of making it harder for young people to be able to become home owners — it might be seen as condemning many young people to renting for most of their lives.

Evaluation of a government subsidy to house builders could be in terms of the opportunity cost of the money spent by government, especially at a time of austerity measures to reduce the budget deficit. Finally, evaluation of an increase in interest rate could come from the impact it could have on the standard of living of existing home borrowers. Many are likely to struggle to repay their monthly house loan and could even end up losing the property, becoming homeless.

Failure to offer any evaluation on all the relevant questions (b, e and g) would limit the student answer to a grade B.

ⓔ Total score: 54/60 marks = grade A

Question 2 Fracking

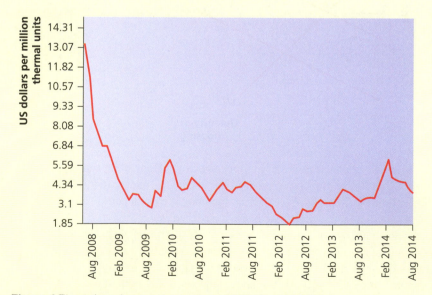

Figure 1 The price of natural gas: June 2008–August 2014

Extract 1 Fracking and the price of gas

Proposals have been made by mining companies to extract vast reserves of underground gas and oil trapped in shale rock that lie beneath many parts of the UK. It involves drilling deep wells and pumping massive quantities of water, sand and chemicals into the rock at high pressure — known as 'fracking'. It releases the gas and oil from the rock, which then rise to the surface for collection.

In the USA, over 40,000 wells have been drilled since 2008 to extract vast quantities of gas and oil. The effect has been dramatic in undermining the global price of gas. Between June 2008 and August 2014 the price of gas fell from $12.68 to $3.88 per metric unit. Fracking now provides around a third of the country's gas supplies and this is expected to rise to more than half by 2035.

Extract 2 The benefits of fracking

Supporters of fracking argue that it provides a vast new energy source that will help keep gas and oil prices down for consumers and reduce the use of coal, which causes even more pollution. In northern England alone there is an estimated 1,300 trillion cubic feet of gas which could supply the country's needs for hundreds of years.

Fracking could lead to private sector investment of £33 billion and create 70,000 jobs over the next 20 years. Firms could potentially make high profits over a long period of time but it is also a high-risk business. Uncertainty exists over the quality of the shale rock and the cost of extraction — in 2014 the mining company Cuadrilla temporarily stopped test drilling for oil in West Sussex.

The central government could gain a substantial amount of corporate tax revenue from fracking companies. Local government could also gain in the areas where fracking takes place. Currently, the companies have offered local communities 1% of the total revenue collected. This could help pay for community projects and reduce other local taxes.

Extract 3 The costs of fracking

Many environmental groups have condemned fracking as a desperate attempt to exploit the last major non-renewable energy resource. In 2012, fracking was temporarily suspended after it caused two minor earthquakes close to Blackpool. There are also long-term fears that property prices will fall in areas where fracking occurs.

Mining companies have attempted to frack in the South Downs National Park, south of London. However, this has been blocked by the park's authority due to fears of its impact on tourism and the environment.

Concern has also been raised over the possibility that fracking might contaminate underground supplies of water with methane and drilling chemicals, which occurred in the USA.

Environmentalists argue that development of renewable energy resources is a cleaner and more sustainable option than reliance on fracked oil and gas.

(a) Refer to Extract 1.

(i) Calculate the percentage change in the price of gas between June 2008 and August 2014.

(2 marks)

e There will often be a quantitative question in the data-response section of the paper. Make sure you can calculate percentages and percentage change from data and explain the results.

(ii) Using the concept of cross elasticity of demand, explain the relationship between the price of gas and demand for coal.

(3 marks)

e Always define key economic concepts used in the question and apply by using information from the extract.

(b) Examine the likely impact on consumer surplus of the change in gas prices between 2008 and 2014. Use a supply and demand diagram in your answer.

(8 marks)

e It is a good idea to show both the original and new equilibrium price and quantities. You need to show the increase in supply from fracking. Also, identify on the diagram the original and new levels of consumer surplus. Remember that an evaluative comment is required to gain the 2 marks available.

(c) With reference to Extract 2, discuss the potential benefits to producers and government following a major expansion of fracking in the UK.

(10 marks)

e It is important that your answer remains focused on the question rather than straying into the benefits for consumers. Use ideas from common sense and also from pointers in the information provided. Remember that up to two evaluative comments are required, as there are 4 marks available for evaluation.

(d) With reference to Extract 3 and the concept of external costs, assess the possible economic effects of widespread fracking in the UK. Use an appropriate diagram in your answer.

(12 marks)

e Make sure you can accurately draw and explain the external cost diagram, identifying the welfare loss triangle in the correct place. This is a crucial part of the syllabus. Remember to offer two evaluative comments as there are 4 marks available for this.

(e) Discuss the effectiveness of taxes and regulations as government measures to reduce market failure from fracking.

(15 marks)

e Make sure you consider both taxes and regulations in order to avoid a mark cap. Diagrammatic analysis is useful when it comes to taxes or regulations, even though the question does not ask for one. Remember to offer at least two evaluative comments as there are 6 evaluation marks available here.

Student answer

(a) (i) $12.68 – $3.88 ÷ $12.68 = –69.4% 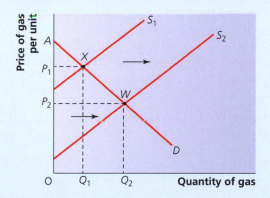 **a**

(ii) Cross elasticity of demand refers to the responsiveness of demand for a good due to a change in price of another good. In this case, we can expect that a fall in price of gas will lead to a fall in demand for coal as they are substitute goods so they have a positive cross elasticity of demand. **b**

e 5/5 marks awarded. a The student calculates the percentage fall in gas price and shows both the workings and a minus sign (2 marks). **b** A definition of cross elasticity of demand is offered with a recognition that substitutes have a positive relationship (1+1 marks), applied to gas and coal (1 mark).

(b) Consumer surplus refers to the difference between the price consumers are prepared to pay for a good and the actual market price paid. **a** Consumer surplus is likely to have increased due to the increase in supply of gas and fall in market price. The diagram shows an increase in supply from S_1 to S_2 and a decrease in price from P_1 to P_2. Consumer surplus increases from area AXP_1 to AWP_2, a rise of P_1XWP_2. **b**

The size of the increase in consumer surplus is likely to be significant due to the large fall in price of gas (69.4%) over the period. However, gas is an essential energy source used for generating electricity, heating and cooking. It is likely that demand will be price inelastic and so consumer surplus may not increase by so much. **c**

e 8/8 marks awarded. a Definition of consumer surplus (1 mark). **b** A correct diagram (3 marks) is supported by an explanation of the original and increase in consumer surplus (2 marks). **c** Evaluation takes the form of the magnitude of price fall and also a comment on the nature of price elasticity of demand for gas (2 marks).

(c) The potential benefits to producers from fracking include high profits over a long period of time. This should lead to an increase in share prices and dividends for companies such as Cuadrilla. High profits also mean higher wages for employees, including bonuses for company directors. If the estimated oil and gas resources prove correct then it could mean long-term security and growth for producers. **a** However, there is a question mark over the economic viability of these resources as Extract 2 points to 'uncertainty over the quality of the shale rock and costs of extraction'. Moreover, one has to take into account strong public opposition to fracking and how a change in government might affect profitability. **b**

The benefits to central government are likely to come from corporate tax revenue (tax on company profits) and the benefits to local government from a share in total company revenues. The former can help reduce the budget deficit and the latter to keep local taxes down, such as business rates and council tax. **c**

e **8/10 marks awarded.** **a** The benefits to producers are well developed, suggesting how high profits could affect company share prices, dividends and salaries (4 marks). **b** Some evaluation is offered, making use of the extract information. There is further development by raising concern over public opposition to fracking and how this might impact on future operations (2 evaluation marks). **c** Potential benefits for central and local government in the form of tax revenue are explained (2 marks). Unfortunately no attempt is made to evaluate this point. Evaluation could come in the form of discussing whether it is such a good deal for government. There is the danger of tax avoidance on company profits, which is easier for foreign mining companies to do. Also a local tax of 1% of total revenues might be too low if the companies proceed to make enormous profits and cause great environmental damage.

(d) External costs are negative third-party effects from a transaction, ignored by the price mechanism. It is the difference between private costs and social costs. **a** Extract 2 points to the possibility of external costs from widespread fracking as seen in the USA. Property prices could fall in the areas close to the fracked wells. They represent a visual eyesore and there may also be air and noise pollution, especially from lorries and pipelines operating nearby. The tourist industry could also be harmed in areas like the South Downs National Park. Even local water supplies could be contaminated by the chemicals used in fracking as in the USA — affecting the water industry and consumers. **b** The diagram shows that the free market equilibrium Q_e exceeds the social optimum of Q_1, leading to a welfare loss of *WXY*. It would be necessary for government to limit the extent of fracking in order to reach the social optimum output where $MSC = MSB$. This will involve charging a higher price for the use of fracked gas from P_e to P_1. **c**

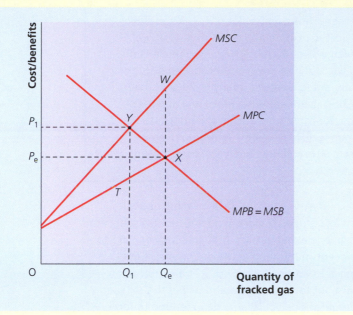

Quantity of fracked gas

ⓔ 8/12 marks awarded. **a** Definition of external costs (1 mark). **b** Good examples of external costs are offered with some development (3 marks). **c** A correct diagram (4 marks) is supported with an explanation of the free market and social optimum equilibrium positions (2 marks). Note a maximum of 8 knowledge, application and analysis marks are available from the 10 marks identified. Unfortunately, no attempt is made to evaluate and so the answer is capped at 8 marks. Evaluation could come in the form of discussing the difficulty in quantifying and attaching a monetary value to external costs. Also some discussion of exactly where the fracked wells would be located is useful — some areas are less sensitive than others. Discussion of benefits from fracking could also be included, so offering balance to the answer.

(e) The government could use different types of taxes to reduce the danger of market failure from fracking. For example, an additional direct tax could be placed on company profits and the money raised used to compensate victims and clean up any damage caused. An indirect tax could also be placed on the sale of fracked gas. **a** However, there are problems with taxation. The government might not use the money raised to compensate victims and instead it could go to reduce the budget deficit. Furthermore, direct taxes may be avoided if companies follow a policy of tax avoidance and indirect taxes are likely to fall more on consumers than producers since gas tends to be price inelastic in demand. Problems also arise over the level of taxes required to internalise the external costs — clearly, information gaps exist over the possible effects of fracking. It might be far better to introduce fracking on an experimental basis in just a few areas for up to ten years to gain more understanding of this energy source. **b**

The government could impose regulations on fracking. This might involve restrictions on the places allowed for drilling and close monitoring of the extraction process to see what effects arise. **c** However, there is no guarantee that regulations will work as the government may lack expertise on fracking compared to the companies involved, many of whom have considerable experience in the USA. Consequently there is a danger of regulatory capture where the government operates in the interests of fracking firms rather than the public. **d** Moreover, regulations can be expensive to monitor and enforce, although it is likely the government could make the firms pay for this anyway.

e **10/15 marks awarded.** **a** Some explanation of taxation is offered, especially distinguishing between direct and indirect taxes (2 marks); an indirect tax diagram would help here to show the effects on price and output. Also it is appropriate to define 'market failure' as this is a concept mentioned in the question. **b** Lots of evaluation is offered on the problems of taxation (2+2 marks). **c** The explanation of regulations is fairly straightforward but lacks analysis and use of the extract information (2 marks). For example, regulations could also be extended to force companies to clean up any damage to the environment and even pay compensation to nearby households for inconvenience caused. Reference could also be made to how regulations may simply block development in environmentally sensitive areas such as the South Downs National Park. **d** A good evaluative comment on regulatory capture is developed (2 marks). This answer has lots of evaluation but lacks analysis.

e **Total score: 39/50 marks = grade B**

Question 3 Open-extended essay

'A minimum price is less effective than taxation to reduce the overconsumption of sugar.'

To what extent do you agree with this statement?   (25 marks)

e The open-extended essay comprises 25% of the total marks available for the A Level paper (25 marks out of a maximum of 100 marks). This means you should spend around half an hour on this question and so need to allocate your time carefully during the exam. The marking is divided into two areas — 16 marks for knowledge, application and analysis, and 9 marks for evaluation.

Knowledge marks can be gained from definitions of minimum prices and indirect taxation; application marks can be gained by using suitable diagrams and offering any evidence from your experiences; analysis marks can be gained by explaining the process by which sugar consumption can be reduced. Evaluation marks can be gained by questioning the extent to which you agree with the statement and, in particular, justifying your decision.

Student answer

The overconsumption of sugar is regarded as a major cause of health problems such as heart disease and diabetes. Many people are overweight and risk ill health which could reduce their quality of life and life expectancy. Various measures have been proposed to reduce the consumption of sugar in diets including a minimum price and taxation. A minimum price represents a legal price floor at which sugar can be sold. Taxation of sugar would be in the form of an indirect tax or expenditure tax on each unit sold. **a**

A minimum price on sugar would have to be set above the free market price in order to have an effect. This is shown in the diagram where the effects are to cause a contraction in demand for sugar from Q_e to Q_1. There might be a temporary extension in supply of sugar from Q_e to Q_2, but this will be short-lived as firms realise an excess supply has been created. This might be an effective way of reducing sugar consumption in goods such sweets, drinks and cakes which now become more expensive and less affordable. It should also encourage companies to reduce the amount of sugar in their products and then market this as a positive step. **b**

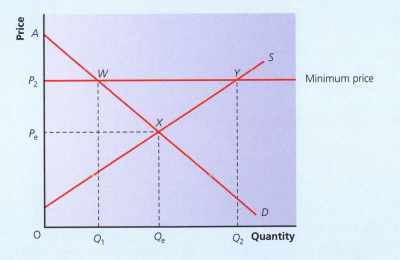

However, there are several limitations to minimum prices that could make it less effective than indirect taxes. Sugar tends to be habit forming and even addictive and so demand is likely to be price inelastic. It means that consumers are likely to still buy sugary foods and drink despite the price rise. Ironically, sugar producers might even gain additional revenue. It could also be difficult for the government to monitor and enforce a minimum price on sugar as it is an ingredient used in a variety of foods and drink. Just how much goes into each product is going to be very hard to work out. **c**

An alternative approach is to impose a specific tax on sugar. It operates in a similar way to minimum pricing in that it will increase the price of sugary goods. The diagram shows the effect of a tax on the sugar market. Output falls from Q_e to Q_1 and price rises from P_e to P_1. There is less consumption of sugar. **d**

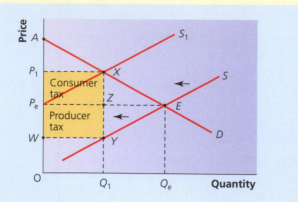

However, there are additional advantages in that it will create tax revenue (area P_1XYW) that the government could then use to fund public health campaigns to warn of the dangers of consuming too much sugar. Treatments could also be funded by the sugar tax and it directly makes consumers and producers pay, helping to internalise external costs. Moreover, taxes work with market forces and so people are still able to buy sugary goods. e

There could be some unintended consequences of sugar taxation. First of all it is a regressive tax and so tends to affect low income groups more than other groups. Sugary foods are already subject to value added tax and companies may believe a further tax is unfair. Another limitation is the danger of an illegal market being created in sugar. However, this is likely to be dependent on the size of the tax. At the end of the day, sugar is quite a low value and bulky product compared to cigarettes and alcohol and so an illegal market is likely to be very limited. f

To conclude, both minimum pricing and taxation have their advantages for reducing sugar consumption. However, the argument seems to favour an indirect tax on sugar since it provides an additional source of revenue for the government to spend on public health campaigns. Minimum prices could also increase revenue for sugar companies if demand proves to be price inelastic. It is for these reasons that the indirect taxation is likely to be more effective in reducing the over-consumption of sugar. g

ⓔ **25/25 marks.** a The introduction explains why overconsumption of sugar is a problem and goes on to define minimum pricing and indirect taxation (4 knowledge marks). b The impact of minimum pricing on the sugar market is explained with good use of a diagram (2 application and 2 analysis marks). c The student considers several limitations of minimum pricing in line with the question (4 analysis marks). d The impact of an indirect tax is explained with good use of a diagram (2 application and 2 analysis marks). e This section considers the advantages of indirect taxation on sugar and counts as evaluation in light of the question (3+3 evaluation marks). f This section now questions the effectiveness of indirect taxation by pointing out some limitations (2 evaluation marks). g A conclusion is offered which confirms the view that taxation is likely to be more effective than minimum pricing in this instance (1 evaluation mark).

Note: Efforts to break down the marks into individual components is rather contrived, especially as examiners will consider the overall quality of the answer in relation to the levels-based mark scheme and whether a suitable structure has been offered. Examiners will expect relevant definitions, diagrams and explanations of how minimum pricing and taxation works. They will also expect at least two and preferably three evaluative comments. All this should be undertaken in the structure of a mini-essay, with an introduction, main body and conclusion.

Knowledge check answers

1 The opportunity cost of you staying on at school to take A Levels is the next best alternative: for example, earning income from a job or joining an apprenticeship scheme to learn a trade.

2 Opportunity cost can be shown by a movement along a production possibility frontier: for example, from position *A* to *B*. An extra 10 units of manufactured goods are obtained at the expense of 5 units of services.

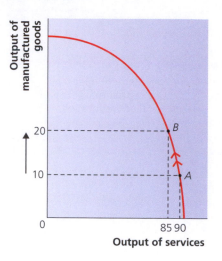

3 There must be unemployed resources in the economy — spare capacity exists.

4 An outward shift of the production possibility frontier might be caused by an increase in the quality or quantity of labour, an increase in capital goods (investment), new technology, enterprise and discovery of natural resources.

5 The division of labour means workers become more skilled at what they do through experience and repetition of tasks. It thereby leads to greater output.

6 The UK is a mixed economy, since both private enterprise and the government decide how resources are allocated for production and distribution.

7 As the price of a good falls, it becomes more affordable for consumers to buy with their income. Also, it becomes relatively cheaper than substitute goods and so some consumers will switch to buying it.

8 A change in the price of the good in question. A rise in price will lead to a contraction in demand and a fall in price will lead to an extension in demand.

9 The main factors include a change in price of substitute or complementary goods and a change in income or tastes. Note that changes in the price of the good will not shift the demand curve.

10 The minus sign means there is an inverse relationship between the change in price and the change in demand. Thus, a rise in price will cause a fall in quantity demanded. The demand curve has a negative gradient.

11 The answer indicates how much a 1% change in price causes demand to change by. For example, an answer of 3 means that a 1% change in price will lead to a 3% change in demand for the good.

12 If a firm knows the price elasticity of demand for the good it produces then it may be able to increase total revenue by changing the price. If demand is inelastic, a rise in price will increase total revenue; if demand is elastic, a fall in price will increase total revenue.

13 If the government knows the price elasticity of demand for a particular good then it will have an idea of the impact that an indirect tax will have on it. For example, a tax placed on a good with inelastic demand should lead to a high tax yield and have relatively little impact on demand.

14 Normal goods have a positive income elasticity of demand; as real income rises, demand for the good also rises. Inferior goods have a negative income elasticity of demand; as real income rises, demand for the good falls.

15 Complementary goods have a negative cross elasticity of demand: for example, a fall in price of computer games consoles will cause an increase in demand for computer games software. Substitute goods have a positive cross elasticity of demand: for example, a rise in price of beef may cause an increase in demand for lamb.

16 As the price of a good rises, there is an incentive to supply more since the firm might achieve higher profits. It is also able to cover the extra costs involved in producing more of the good.

17 A change in the price of the good in question. A rise in price will lead to an extension in supply and a fall in price will lead to a contraction in supply.

18 The main factors include a change in costs of production, technology, the ability of firms to enter and exit an industry, indirect taxes and government subsidies. Note that changes in the price of the good will not shift the supply curve.

19 A positive number means there is a direct relationship between the change in price and the change in quantity supplied. Thus, a rise in price will cause a rise in the quantity supplied. The supply curve has a positive gradient.

20 The figure indicates by how much a 1% change in price causes quantity supplied to change. For example, an answer of 2 means that a 1% change in price will lead to a 2% change in quantity supplied of the good.

21 For most goods, supply tends to be relatively price inelastic in the short run as some factor inputs are fixed in quantity, but becomes relatively price elastic in the long run when all factor inputs are variable.

22 If supply exceeds demand, price will fall, leading to an extension in demand and a contraction in supply. Eventually, equilibrium position is reached.

23 If demand exceeds supply, price will rise, leading to an extension in supply and contraction in demand. Eventually, equilibrium position is reached.

24 A decrease in demand for a good will cause its price to fall and so lead to a decrease in producer surplus and consumer surplus.

25 A decrease in supply of a good will cause price to rise but a fall in both the consumer surplus and producer surplus.

26 A specific tax is placed as a fixed amount per unit of good and causes an inward parallel shift in the supply curve. An *ad valorem* tax is placed as a percentage of the price of a good and causes an inward pivotal shift in the supply curve.

27 A unit subsidy will shift the supply curve outwards (an increase in supply) and reduce the equilibrium price.

28 Alternative views of consumer behaviour are those which assume consumers do not always aim or behave in a way that maximises total utility from their expenditure.

29 Consumers may not maximise total utility due to: copying other consumers rather than thinking for themselves; keeping with their habits rather than making changes; difficulties in computation.

30 Social costs are the total of private costs and external costs.

31 Social benefits are the total of private benefits and external benefits.

32 Market equilibrium is the output position where marginal private benefits (*MPB*) equal marginal private costs (*MPC*). Externalities are ignored. However, the social optimum is where marginal social benefits (*MPB*) equal marginal social costs (*MPC*).

33 The welfare loss triangle is the area on an externality diagram that depicts the excess of social costs over social benefits for a given level of output.

34 The welfare gain triangle is the area on an externality diagram that depicts the excess of social benefits over social costs for a given output level.

35 External costs cause market failure since they are ignored by the price mechanism and lead to a welfare loss. For example, a person smoking leads to passive smoking for others, who suffer but are not compensated.

36 External benefits cause market failure since they are ignored by the price mechanism and lead to a loss of potential welfare. For example, a person paying for a vaccination will reduce the risk of disease for others but this benefit is not accounted for by the price mechanism and so underprovision occurs.

37 On a hot day a public beach might become so overcrowded that people compete for space on the beach — there may be rivalry in consumption. A public

beach might also be sold off to a property developer who restricts access to members of the public.

38 The free-rider problem is where an individual is able to consume a good without paying for it. Consequently, there is no incentive for firms to supply the good in a free market.

39 Public goods are a type of market failure since there would be no provision or very little provision of them in a free market. This is due to the free-rider problem — where it is possible to consume the goods without paying for them. Consequently, there is no profit incentive for firms to provide them.

40 Imperfect market information leads to market failure because consumers and producers may make decisions on buying or selling a good which reduce their overall welfare.

41 The key reason for government intervention is to correct market failure so that markets work more efficiently and there is less welfare loss.

42 High taxes are placed on tobacco, alcohol and petrol in order to internalise external costs. They are a way of making the polluters pay for these costs. In addition, they provide significant tax revenue to the government, since demand is typically price inelastic for these goods.

43 The government typically subsidises goods which have significant external benefits in production or consumption: for example, renewable energy sources, public transport and healthcare.

44 A maximum price in the house rental sector will help low-income families afford to rent property and reduce the danger of exploitation.

45 Maximum price controls may reduce both the supply and quality of rental housing, leading to a greater shortage in the market.

46 A minimum price for alcohol and sugar will reduce the costs associated with these products: for example, crime, alcoholism, obesity, pressure on the healthcare service and absenteeism from work.

47 Disadvantages include the danger of shadow markets being formed as well as increasing the price of goods for low-income households.

48 A 'cap and trade' scheme is where the government limits the amount of pollution that firms are able to emit but also allows them to buy and sell pollution permits between themselves.

49 A system of tradable pollution permits was introduced in order to limit pollution emissions from heavy industry. The EU believes that by creating a market for pollution it can help reduce overall carbon emissions.

50 If too many pollution permits are issued then the price falls so much that there is little incentive for firms to cut back on emissions; if too few permits are issued then the price of permits rises so much as to make EU industry uncompetitive in global markets.

Index